P9-BBV-675

101 KEY IDEAS

Existentialism

Also available in the series

101 KEY IDEAS

Existentialism

George Myerson

TEACH YOURSELF BOOKS

For UK order queries: please contact Bookpoint Ltd, 39 Milton Park, Abingdon, Oxon OX14 4TD. Telephone: (44) 01235 400414, Fax: (44) 01235 400454. Lines are open from 9.00–6.00, Monday to Saturday, with a 24 hour message answering service. Email address: orders@bookpoint.co.uk

For USA & Canada order queries: please contact NTC/Contemporary Publishing, 4255 West Touhy Avenue, Lincolnwood, Illinois 60646–1975, USA. Telephone: (847) 679 5500, Fax: (847) 679 2494.

Long renowned as the authoritative source for self-guided learning – with more than 30 million copies sold worldwide – the *Teach Yourself* series includes over 200 titles in the fields of languages, crafts, hobbies, business and education.

British Library Cataloguing in Publication Data
A catalogue record for this title is available from The British Library.

Library of Congress Catalog Card Number: On file

First published in UK 2000 by Hodder Headline Plc, 338 Euston Road, London, NW1 3BH.

First published in US 2000 by NTC/Contemporary Publishing, 4255 West Touhy Avenue, Lincolnwood (Chicago), Illinois 60646–1975 USA.

Cover illustration and design by Mike Stones.

Typeset by Transet Limited, Coventry, England.
Printed in Great Britain for Hodder & Stoughton Educational, a division of Hodder Headline Plc, 338 Euston Road, London NW1 3BH by Cox & Wyman Ltd, Reading, Berkshire.

Impression number   10 9 8 7 6 5 4 3 2
Year   2005 2004 2003 2002 2001 2000

Contents

Introduction

Welcome to the **Teach Yourself 101 Key Ideas** series. We hope that you will find both this book and others in the series to be useful, interesting and informative. The purpose of the series is to provide an introduction to a wide range of subjects, in a way that is entertaining and easy to absorb.

Each book contains 101 short accounts of key ideas or terms which are regarded as central to that subject. The accounts are presented in alphabetical order for ease of reference. All of the books in the series are written in order to be meaningful whether or not you have previous knowledge of the subject. They will be useful to you whether you are a general reader, are on a pre-university course, or have just started at university.

We have designed the series to be a combination of a text book and a dictionary. We felt that many text books are too long for easy reference, while the entries in dictionaries are often too short to provide sufficient detail. The **Teach Yourself 101 Key Ideas** series gives the best of both worlds! Here are books that you do not have to read cover to cover, or in any set order. Dip into them when you need to know the meaning of a term, and you will find a short, but comprehensive account which will be of real help with those essays and assignments. The terms are described in a straightforward way with a careful selection of academic words thrown in for good measure!

So if you need quick and inexpensive introduction to a subject, **Teach Yourself 101 Key Ideas** is for you. And incidentally, if you have any suggestions about this book or the series, do let us know. It would be great to hear from you.

Best wishes with your studies!

Paul Oliver
Series Editor

To my son, Simon,
philosophically and with love.

Absurd

'That's absurd!' we say, when we think something could not possibly happen; or if an idea or argument has no connection with reality; or if something has happened but still doesn't make any sense, and can't be taken seriously. It is a gesture of dismissal. In Existentialism, the absurd is turned on its head, and becomes the principle of reality instead of its opposite, the criterion of relevance instead of its opposite. The existential idea of the absurd was taken furthest by Camus, who proclaimed it with almost religious fervour: 'From the moment the absurd is recognized, it becomes a passion'. And this passion, like religious intensity, is 'harrowing'.

What did Camus mean, when he talked of recognizing the absurd? Sometimes, he takes a provocatively intense and gloomy approach, defining this absurd quality as 'the primitive hostility of the world'. Most of the time, we carry on unaware of the world around us. Then suddenly, a certain 'denseness and strangeness' breaks in upon us. It is the reverse of the usual idea of illumination or inspiration. This absurdity is a kind of negative illumination. At a certain moment, we see that we really cannot make any sense of the most obvious and familiar things in our lives.

Take an ordinary object, such as the carpet we walk over every day of our lives down the corridor at work. This day I notice it, the blue pattern, the stains, the frayed edges. And then I look out of the window and see an ambulance tearing down the street, siren blaring. I can't put these sensations together, and yet I do so every second of every day to make up the ordinary texture that I call everyday life. How can that old coffee stain by my foot share the same world as that desperate wailing siren, and inside the ambulance the last drama of a person I have never known, will never know, yet who shares with me the consciousness of that blaring sound? That is the absurd, that sensation of the impossibility of these things belonging together.

see also...

Anxiety; World

Action

Action poses Existentialism some of its greatest problems. Whatever their differences, Existentialists do not seek to turn people away from the world: there is no existential salvation in simply standing apart from life, being passive, contemplating things from as far away as you can get. In the words of Paul Tillich, the self 'must act because it lives'. We are not offered the possibility of abstaining indefinitely from action. Eventually, if you sit thinking about what to do for long enough, your indecision becomes an act, or even a whole life.

A child is crying in the street. Once I notice, I have become involved in the situation. The world offers itself to me as a choice of actions: to walk past, to watch and see, to go over and ask what's wrong, to call a policeman. But each option rules out more than it enacts: in each case, the number of things I could have done is infinitely larger than whatever I have chosen. Tillich defines the dilemma: 'Acting involves him who acts in that upon which he acts'. Whatever I decide, I have surrendered an immense range of other possibilities, many of which might well have been better, better for me and for others. To act means to give up my freedom, to become bound to the situation in a certain way. But I have no way of not acting: the world has put me in a position which makes everything into an action, watching as much as speaking, walking by as much as going over.

You might say that freedom is pointless if you don't ever choose to act. But, then again, all action loses you far more than it gains, in terms of possibilities. Sartre's hero Mathieu has lived a life of trying to avoid decisive actions, and in the end he stands on a hill, surrounded by Nazi soldiers and as he pulls the trigger of his gun he feels he is acting for the first time. Then darkness descends on him, and every possibility seems ended.

see also...

Decision; Possibility

Address

The easiest way to explain language is to imagine it as a vast collection of names, labels we can stick to things and people. In this version of language and life, each person roams through the world attaching words as firmly as possible. The story begins in Genesis, where Adam names all the animals, and so gets a grip on both language and the world in one fell swoop. By contrast, Existentialism views language less as a way of naming the world than as a way of entering into relationships. The concept of 'Address' is important for talking about this language of relationship.

Existentialism resists general definitions of 'humanity' or general rules of conduct. But one of the ways you can tell you are in the presence of an equivalent being to yourself is that you will feel the need to 'address' her, to talk to her rather than merely about her, and indeed to orient your whole behaviour towards her rather than just doing something about her. As the philosopher Martin Heidegger put it, where human beings are concerned, there is always a 'mineness' in action, they too are experiencing a life as 'my life'. It is this 'mineness' that you feel the need to address, to call out towards: 'I am', 'You are'. Language embodies this drive to address and be addressed. The existential Genesis begins not with naming but with conversation.

Religious Existentialists did discover such a conversation at the origin of human existence in the world. For the Jewish theologian Martin Buber, 'God addresses man and is addressed by him'. The naming of the animals isn't the birth of language; what matters is the first call from God to man, a call to which a reply is expected. God does not set the human world in motion by naming people, but by calling upon them. We are not spoken for, but we have been spoken to: and living is the process of responding to the call, the address. To address means to want a reply: to be addressed means to want to reply.

see also...

I; Presence

Ambiguity

A family is sitting round the dining-table, three children with two adults. Each is participating from their own perspective in making the family and the occasion. Each is also aware of the others alongside, externally. Then again, the scene exists within each of them, distinctly and definitely, as they each exist for themselves. Twenty years later, they will remember these kinds of occasion, each in their own perspective. For some it may be a memory of togetherness, for others it may be about concealment or loss.

There is what de Beauvoir calls a 'fundamental ambiguity' about human life, enacted in this scene and in every other. Each person feels their life as 'inwardness', the unfolding of a story visible only to them. But each is also aware of that same life in terms of 'externality'. There is an outside to that personal inside. One may remember one's past inwardly, but equally the others have their memories of you, from the outside. You cannot give a conclusive meaning to your own life. Yes, you may remember the dinner-table as cosy togetherness; but how do the others recall it – and you?

De Beauvoir transformed Existentialism into what she called, in the title of a book, *The Ethics of Ambiguity*. The double existence – inward and external – was also conceived by Sartre, Heidegger and, before them, Dostoyevsky and Kierkegaard. But de Beauvoir gave it a particular emphasis. She urged that we 'try to assume our fundamental ambiguity': that we live out fully this recognition of the inner and outer manifestations of our lives. Experienced inwardly, life is always in the process of 'making itself'. Conversely, from the outside the same life is there as a fact in the world.

For de Beauvoir, the refusal to live with fundamental ambiguity is the origin of much that is oppressive and authoritarian. Those in flight from their own ambiguity need to suppress the perspectives of many other people. They are the world's 'serious people', they can tolerate no questioning of their important truths, such as the sacredness of the happy family.

see also...

Others; Questions

Anguish

I am about to make a very important telephone call. My fingers are pushing the buttons for the number. Any minute and I will be through, and the call will have begun. In my mind, I have already prepared what I want to say. My thoughts have already cast themselves ahead into that future moment, so that I am not really conscious of the present. There is only one digit left: my finger is over that button. Now it suddenly strikes me: I am not yet there, I could still choose not to make the call. In my mind, I was already inside a future in which the connection has occurred; now I glimpse another future me, who has put the phone down without connecting.

I pause briefly, and in an ordinary way I might call this a touch of indecision. But this could also be a moment when existential 'anguish' comes to the surface. Such anguish is the particular feeling you have when life seems to be suspended in time. You are caught hanging between a future idea which has already absorbed you and a present which is not that future. In between there is a gulf, empty of both present and future. This gulf is a kind of freedom and also a peculiar emptiness.

Sartre defines anguish as 'my consciousness of being my own future, in the mode of non-being.' Anguish comes from our sense of ourselves as being in time. I will still be me when I say 'hello': after all, that is why I am interested in the idea. As Sartre says, 'I am already what I will be'. Yet it is equally the case that I am not the person who has made the call: I still have to cross the space in which I could turn aside from that future me. In ordinary indecision I hesitate and go on, or back. In anguish I feel as if I no longer exist: my life falls into the empty space which is between the anticipation and the act.

see also...

Nothing; Time

Anxiety

Existentialism is a philosophy of emotions, and often of apparently negative ones, like anxiety. Everyone has worries. If you want to understand what somebody is doing, you often have to know what he or she is worrying about. Why did I shout at the driver in front who wouldn't keep going through that amber light: because I need to get to work early so that I can see if I can find the letter which is worrying me. But there is something beyond these ordinary worries. Sometimes, we reach a state of mind which goes beyond this worry or that worry. Nothing we do brings peace of mind now. One worry gives way immediately to another, and we can see, in a sudden glimpse, that all the specific worries are moving over the surface of a bigger feeling. Martin Heidegger calls this indefinable worry anxiety, and he says: 'That in the face of which one is anxious is completely indefinite.' Suddenly, we catch ourselves out and know that we aren't really worrying about whether we locked the door as we left home this morning, or whether the boss will be angry about the late memo. Anxiety is worry which has unhooked itself from the little, real-life reasons. Anxiety just won't go away, and yet it won't tell us what the matter is either.

Heidegger believes that such anxiety is a sudden sharp feeling of the existence of the world, nothing more or less than that: 'the world as such is that in the face of which one has anxiety'. This seems a very strange idea; so Heidegger points out that we are often quite aware, in fact, that our anxiety is empty: 'What oppresses us ... is the world itself. When anxiety has subsided, then in our everyday way of talking we are accustomed to say that "it was really nothing".' In these bursts of anxiety, the ordinariness of things is lost, and we experience the strangeness of everything, and of ourselves: 'Everyday familiarity collapses.' Anxiety reminds us that, as Existentialism insists, we don't have answers to the big questions.

see also...

Emotion; Reasons

Appearances

You go into a busy café. You are greeted by a host of objects, all wreathed in smoke and the buzz of noise and music. Cups and plates rattle, food steams and smokes. Among these objects, also in the haze, are people, engaged in various dramas and the semi-public performances of themselves that are appropriate in this setting. What then is it you are seeing and sensing, as you take it all in?

For Sartre, what appears for you is what there is. There is nothing hidden behind or within these appearances as they greet your different senses. Of course, it is in the nature of such appearances that they present themselves to a point of view; you are absorbing the café scene from your position and with your expectations. Maybe, as Sartre speculates, you are hoping to see a friend, in which case you may notice his absence, a feature invisible to anyone else. That is how the world arises for us, as appearances greeting a point of view. But this does not make the appearances in any way insubstantial or illusory. There is no real café somewhere behind the one you think you are

entering. In Sartre's existential terms, 'The appearance does not hide the essence, it reveals it; it *is* the essence.'

But not everyone is happy to endorse appearances as fully as this. One could object, for instance, to the idea that people are revealed by their appearance just like the rest of the café. The Catholic Existentialist Maritain tried to rescue existence from Sartre's appearance world. For Maritain, this café would epitomize a false view of 'the chaos of slimy and disaggregated appearances'. With no inner meaning, everything simply slides from moment to moment of a 'finite existence', and we make our lives from mere 'images launched into time.' With all his revulsion, Maritain sees an important aspect of Sartre's vision: no idea connects all the appearances, unless we choose to create one for ourselves. Of course, Sartre would reply that only someone falsely expecting coherence would be disappointed by this infinite play of appearance.

see also...

Christian Existentialism; Reality

Atheism

You could divide Existentialists into those whose philosophy finds no place for any god, and the others. The godless ones include: Sartre, de Beauvoir, Nietzsche, Beckett, Kundera, Camus. The others might be: Tillich, Buber, Auden, Jaspers, Berdyaev, Maritain, Marcel, Kierkegaard, Dostoevsky. There would be tricky cases, notably Heidegger.

This divide could be expressed in different ways. The godless ones themselves do not usually present themselves as primarily denying the traditional beliefs. They have, in their terms, left that language behind. For example, Samuel Beckett is not denying God when he creates plays and fables where people crawl through an empty universe, bumping into the remains of existence as they go. He has simply presented the world without reference to any idea about God.

However, religious Existentialists firmly define themselves by contrast with what they see as the atheism of the dominant current in the movement. The Catholic Maritain argues against 'the initial decision and hygienic bias of Existentialism:

manage at all costs to make atheism liveable'. For Maritain, Existentialism has itself made a commitment to identify with modern atheism, a choice which then gets passed over and treated as an inevitability. Thus, he would say, thinkers like Nietzsche and Sartre have concealed the active commitment they have made to the atheist viewpoint. They have treated it as a natural starting point, when in fact it is a decision. So Maritain argues that atheism has been the moment of deep betrayal for Existentialism, the disowning of freedom.

An alternative analysis of this existential atheism was developed by the Russian Orthodox thinker Berdyaev, who contrasted an earlier phase of atheism with the new existential variety. The old atheism was founded on science, on enlightenment, the hope of human perfectibility. The new atheism is based on despair. But this too is a choice, which Berdyaev believes could be undone without undermining existential principles.

see also...

Christian Existentialism; God

Authenticity

Human beings have no way to experience *life* in general. We can only experience *my* life. Even something as absolute as the sky can only be grasped within my life; we still share this sky, but each from within our own life. So if I try to think about what a life is, I can only imagine it on the basis of my life. Growing up involves the difficult realization that others too must be living a life which is *mine*.

Yet often people try to live as if they had dispensed with the *my* in their life. From this follows one of the big distinctions in Existentialism, made most forcefully by Heidegger. To try to renounce this 'mineness' of life is to enter into a condition which he calls 'inauthenticity'. Conversely, to acknowledge fully the 'mineness' of your life is to live with authenticity. Authenticity and inauthenticity are both, for Heidegger, 'modes of being', that is they are ways of belonging to the world. If you are in an authentic condition, then you start from 'my life': you see the sky clearly as 'my sky', coloured by 'my' feelings and associations. Only then can you fully acknowledge that the others also have 'my' sky in view, grasped just as

personally. Then you can see how the sky is real to each of us; we can begin a true dialogue of experience. Inauthenticity allows no such dialogue. Instead, it tries to blot out all differences. This experience is not *our* sky, for that is just a way of saying *mine* with others. The truly inauthentic 'mode' is what Sartre calls 'the they'. It means experiencing the sky as belonging not to me, not to us, but to them, of whom I am facelessly one.

We have all experienced the breeze of relief you can feel when you close the door behind you on your own life, and walk into the impersonal street: you can kid yourself for a moment you are one of them, not a me but a they. The relief is what Existentialists mean by inauthenticity.

see also...

Existential Position; I

Bad Faith

Lies and illusions are major themes in Existentialism. For Existentialists, people often reveal their identity most vividly in the lies they tell, and particularly in the lies they tell to themselves. One of the most important existential ideas is Bad Faith, which is Sartre's name for the state of mind in which we lie to ourselves. Some of these inner lies are trivial: I know that I am going to be late if I don't go now, but I carry on as if I think there is plenty of time. Then I am in Bad Faith: I am being deliberately late, but I allow myself to believe I am unaware of it. When you complain, I can say: 'My goodness, I never noticed the time.' Sartre points out how weird this self-deception is: '…the one to whom the lie is told and the one who lies are one and the same person'. The liar is also the victim. In Bad Faith, I am pretending to be two different people; I am myself, but I am also another person. Neither is responsible for how I seem to have acted.

But the real trouble about Bad Faith isn't little moments of self-deception. Existentialism is about whole ways of living, choices of life, and Bad Faith can infect an entire life. As Sartre puts it, in sadness and in anger: 'A person can live in bad faith.' You can spend your whole life as if you weren't the person you really are. So there can be a vicious gaoler who feels he is a truly kind and sympathetic person; there can be a bully who is sure she is tolerant and easy-going. Bad Faith is the secret of such lives, the willing victim is ever-ready to believe their own lie. Bad Faith is a way of 'establishing that I am not what I am'. If the lie really works, then when other people confront me with my actions, I will genuinely feel disbelief and outrage. This concept of Bad Faith is an example of the wider existential idea, that nothing can relieve us of the burden of responsibility for our lives and our actions.

see also...

Lies; Responsibility

de Beauvoir, Simone

Simone de Beauvoir (1908–86) was a leading French novelist and philosopher, a major influence on the twentieth-century development of both Existentialism and feminism. Her first major publication was the novel *She Came To Stay* (1943), which explored the impact of a young woman in the life of a couple, a situation derived from her own life with Jean-Paul Sartre. De Beauvoir's relationship with Sartre, complex and ambiguous, was central to the redevelopment of Existentialism in France. As the influential feminist critic Judith Butler notes, de Beauvoir contributed her own specific themes and tones to this existential movement. Her major writings most closely associated with Existentialism include: *The Blood of Others* (1945), a novel set in the time of the French resistance; *The Ethics of Ambiguity* (1947), an existential theory of identity and choice; and *The Second Sex* (1949), a major study of the position, oppression and liberation of women.

De Beauvoir contributed one of the most influential sentences to twentieth century thought when, in *The Second Sex*, she wrote: 'One is not born, but rather becomes, a woman.' Donna Haraway, a leading thinker in contemporary American feminism and cultural theory, sees this sentence as at the heart of the evolution of the modern feminist movement. The emphasis on becoming, as against fixed essences and qualities, serves to connect de Beauvoir's idea with Existentialism.

According to Iris Murdoch, de Beauvoir's vision was most profoundly shaped by the experience of the Nazi occupation. For Murdoch, de Beauvoir reinterpreted both Existentialism and everyday life in terms of the urgent dilemmas and decisions of a Resistance movement. *The Blood of Others* is exemplary, exploring the French defeat of 1940, through the eyes and mind of Jean Blomart, bourgeois, trade union leader and now Resistance organizer. He is watching his lover, Hélène, dying. What does it mean to be free in such a world?

see also...

Ambiguity; Essence

Beckett, Samuel

Samuel Beckett (1906–89) was a major writer in English and in French, in prose fiction and drama. Though born near Dublin, and educated in Ireland, Beckett became a world-renowned figure after he moved to France in 1937. He was a member of the French Resistance during the war. Beckett's most famous work was written in French and then translated, usually by himself, into English. This includes the dramas *Waiting For Godot* (1952/54) and *Endgame (1956/57)*, works which were central to what Martin Esslin termed 'the theatre of the absurd'. Hugh Kenner, watching Beckett direct a later work, *Play*, in 1964 felt that as Beckett called for the lights to fade he was holding out the hope, or prospect, of non-existence. This trembling on the edge of nothingness is characteristic of Beckett's plays, from the moment when *Godot* begins with the announcement 'Nothing to be done'. In *Endgame*, the play is punctuated by announcements that one after another things are disappearing, humble everyday objects and also more resonant things like painkillers. These plays are physical equivalents to many of the ideas also explored by existential thought: nothingness, loss, the burden of endless choice, the weight of the body, the ambiguity of being both corporeal and mental, the twists and tricks of time passing.

Beckett was also a major prose writer. Before the great plays, he wrote, for example, a mysterious series of novels including *Watt*, written during the war in 1944–5, *Malone Dies* (1947–8 in French, 1958 in English), and *The Unnameable* (1953/58). In *Watt*, the main character Watt exists in relation to the shadowy power of Mr Knott: existence confronts negation, the existential predicament. Watt moves from dilemma to dilemma: will he sit down first, or put down his bags; will he close the door first, or sit down? In his later prose, these fundamental situations of existence are even more nakedly depicted. In *Texts for Nothing* (1954/67) a struggling 'I' tries to find a voice, always outwitted by the puzzles of time: 'for the moment I am here', he declares, and then 'always have been'.

see also...

Body; Nothing

Becoming

There are many things I cannot become, however hard I try, however much I wish. I am not going to be a rock star, or an international footballer, or a great scientist. To live as if I could become any of these things would be mere delusion. Am I then fixed, destined to be the person I am and nothing else? Is living with one's eyes open always a matter of accepting limits?

Yet, for Existentialism there is something fundamentally false about the apparent realism and honesty of accepting limitations. The falseness can best be seen by thinking about the very beginning of our life. Yes, says psychiatrist and philosopher R D Laing, there is 'physical birth', but this birth stops far short of the beginning of a human life. Amazingly, there soon follows a process of expansion, by which 'the infant feels real and alive'. The baby needs to become alive, from its own point of view. Without this becoming, the first birth is empty. So our life began in a leap of becoming, a leap which you might say was completely unrealistic. If the small infant accepted its limits, there would never be a chance of experiencing life whole and from a strong centre of self. We are ourselves by virtue of a great jump of becoming.

To understand yourself, or someone else as a person, means not only to define what is already there but to grasp 'what it is possible for him to become', in the terms of Karl Jaspers. If you want to understand anything about a newborn baby, you need to recognize, as we almost all do, what is possible, what the new 'organism' can become. With older people it gets harder to see the potential becoming, yet it is as much a real part of their life as in the case of the newborn baby.

see also...

Creativity; Lack

Being

A baby is lying on the carpet. She is obviously looking, her feet and arms are waving. Here comes a hand into her field of vision, behind the hand there seems to be an interesting noise. Now there is a thing in view, held by that hand: you can see the eyes widen, the hands flutter, the feet jiggle. Then you say helpfully: 'It's a car!' But what has the baby been seeing? The excitement was present through her whole body, she had caught sight of what you see as a car. But she has no ideas about cars, or toy cars, and she has no words for the red colour or the shiny look.

In existential terms, the baby sees a little chunk of being, a chunk to which she can give no definition that we would recognize. Yet she does know all sorts of things about being, long before she knows about cars or toys or even hands. She knows these chunks of being are sharing the world with her: she is becoming aware of herself in relation to them. Indeed, if she is small enough, her own feet also look like interesting bits of being! In Heidegger's terms, Being is 'that on the basis of which entities are already understood', however we

may discuss them in detail. The baby has a good understanding already of the world as a place in which she encounters being, not as one great abstract envelope, but in lots of little entities, some more stable than others.

Babies don't need Heidegger to explain being to them. They are busy recognizing 'that which determines entities as entities', long before they are interested in understanding this one as a toy red car, that one as a plastic purple house. Before you can think about what makes this a toy house, that a toy car, you have to open your eyes to the fact of their being. It is, in Heidegger's terms, a task of Existentialism 'to make the being of entities stand out in full relief' for us once more, including our own being.

see also...

Equipment; Objects

Betrayal

Existentialists have have been fascinated by betrayal, of individuals, of causes, of countries, of humanity, of gods. Kierkegaard sees the biblical Abraham and Isaac as a story of paternal betrayal, just as much as of miraculous faith: if Abraham had told the truth to Isaac – that he was going to be a sacrificial offering – he would never have got the chance to display his faith to God by sacrificing the boy, until saved by the angel. And Kierkegaard's other great examples include *The Diary of a Seducer*. Camus is fascinated by Don Juan; Sartre writes of partners who betray one another, friends who deceive one another. Double agents and con men haunt existential fiction and philosophy.

What is the interest of betrayal? In his famous novel, *The Unbearable Lightness of Being,* Milan Kundera includes a 'Dictionary of Misunderstood Words', and among them are 'Fidelity and Betrayal'. In practice, he concentrates on the negative. In his novel, betrayal is associated with a young woman called Sabine, who has left Czechoslovakia to suffer the Russian invasion of 1968 in her absence, while she has an affair and becomes an artist in Geneva. She has always been told that betrayal is a terrible thing, that loyalty is a great virtue. But she refuses to accept this lesson of her father and all the other authorities. For Sabine, betrayal is a supreme act because it 'means breaking ranks'. Only in the moment of betrayal does she feel she is choosing for herself, breaking out of the definitions imposed by others. Betrayal is committed alone, it is the pure act of the isolated individual. As she passes from one lover to another, one home to another, she is alone with her own will.

Yet there is a deeper problem about betrayal: it is endless. As Sabine senses, once she has completed one betrayal, she longs for the next. Therefore, in the end 'emptiness was the goal of all her betrayal'. This emptiness is the unbearable lightness of being: a world and a life to which no purpose can stick, the dark side of freedom.

see also...

Cynicism; Lies

Body

Although it sounds odd, you can speak of your experience of your own body. There are certain situations in which you don't notice your body, but rather use it as a means of attending to the world. But in other situations, the body itself can become the focus of experience. It's the difference between walking down the street and sinking into a warm bath. As you head for the shops, you are experiencing the outside world through your body: as you enter the water, you are experiencing your body through the contact with that environment. There is something quite strange about this everyday ability to treat the body as either an experience in itself or merely a medium for gaining information about the outside.

Existentialism has consistently explored the body as a process, rather than merely an object. Perhaps the most graphic examples come from the work of Samuel Beckett. In one story, he has a character tell us his changing experience of the body in a kind of running commentary: 'I say to the body, Up with you now, and I can feel it struggling' *(Texts for Nothing)*. This experience of the body as resistance to the will is another way to define what it means to be tired. Tiredness is a way of being with my body, of feeling its obdurate refusal to fit in. Later, the same character seeks comfort in a wave of desolate loneliness: 'I'm in my arms, I'm holding myself in my arms.' Here sadness itself becomes a certain experience of my body, as something vulnerable, small, in need of support. There is also the strange way in which we can imagine our own bodily existence as if it were not ours: 'Imagine hands … Imagine hands'.

We only experience our own being in terms of this body. De Beauvoir has a speaker who reaches towards death first as 'no longer to know anything'. But finally her character sees that this will be a dead body when it is no longer known from within. In death, the body's weight will not be felt.

see also...

Emotion; Touch

16

Buber, Martin

Martin Buber (1878–1965) was a major figure in German philosophy, Jewish faith and twentieth-century religious thought. He was most widely known for *I and Thou* (1923), a work which makes rich connections between German philosophy and Jewish tradition. Buber became associated particularly with the Jewish school known as 'hasidism', and at the same time his influence spread among many Christian and secular thinkers. He also engaged deeply with Eastern and Chinese spirituality, making him a figure of world spirituality in modern times. Buber's other works include: *Talks and Parables of Chung Tzu* (1910), *The Holy Way* (1918), *The Prophetic Faith* (1942) and *The Dialogue Between Heaven and Earth* (1951).

In his work on Chung Tzu's Taoism, Buber writes of our life as stretching out 'from the solitude of the abyss to the solitude of the sea'. He participates deeply in the existential encounter with nothingness, absence and the anguish of unrelieved choice.

At the heart of Buber's work is the encounter with the other, a fellow human being and also perhaps God. The Christian theologian Don Cupitt sums up Buber's teaching: 'in one's experience of a fellow human-being there is something immeasurable, ultimate, and so implicitly theological'. This reflection upon 'otherness' makes Buber's work important to Existentialism. In *I and Thou*, Buber imagines himself standing by a tree. He can see it as a picture, or a movement, or he can feel its presence in his world. He can dissipate that presence, or he can enter into an ever-deepening recognition. From here, Buber goes on to consider the universal situation where he faces a human being. Again, the question is how to recognize this other being. From here the thought moves to the dialogue with God. In the face of modern history, where God seemed absent, Buber persisted with this dialogue.

see also...
Address; Dialogue

Camus, Albert

Albert Camus (1913–60) was born in French Algeria, which provides the setting for his single most famous work, the novel *The Outsider*. This work, together with the influential essays *The Myth of Sisyphus* (apart from a section later added on Kafka) appeared in Paris in 1942 during the Nazi occupation. During this period, Camus joined a resistance group known as Combat, for whom he edited an underground journal. By 1950, Iris Murdoch could count Camus as one of the leading figures in Existentialism, even if Camus himself was not happy with the term itself. After the war, Camus' work includes the novels *The Plague* (1947) and *The Fall* (1956), and the influential work of argument and polemic *The Rebel* (1951). Camus was through this period involved in a complex public and private dialogue with Sartre and de Beauvoir. There were many shared questions, but also many different answers among the three, and Camus differed most strongly with Sartre over the latter's affiliation with Marxism. For Iris Murdoch, however, their work evoked a similar sense that the meaning had vanished from human experience, notably in Sartre's *Nausea* and Camus' *The Outsider*. The 'outsider', Mersault, commits what is judged to be the crime of murder under the bitter glare of the mid-day sun, whose light seems to deprive the world of all depth and significance.

Murdoch saw Rieux, hero of *The Plague*, as the perfect existential hero. He confronts the horrors of plague-ridden Oran with perfect clarity, and his lack of illusion is never an excuse of inaction – nor was it with Camus himself during and after the war. In *The Fall*, the one who has fallen, one-time lawyer Jean-Baptiste Clamence, spins a sequence of caustic sayings out of his despair. Acknowledging his many failings and worse, he notes that everyone is 'exceptional', to himself. For the critic Roland Barthes in the 1950s, Camus seemed a conservative influence, emphasizing isolation; for Walter Kaufman, Camus was self-deluded, never able to achieve the indifference he seemed to urge on others. Yet Camus' heroes retain a mythic force. He won the Nobel Prize in 1957.

see also...

Absurd; Sisyphus

Chance

Why are are so many of us keen on astrology? Why are there so many horoscopes, and why is it that even cynics like me cast an eye over the predictions? Astrological predictions mainly cover events which we would otherwise see as chance, good or bad luck. You will have a lucky meeting; your finances will suddenly improve; you may meet the love of your life. Astrology takes what seem to be chance happenings and returns them to the universe of pattern and logic, of meaning. We tend to see chance as a gap in the fabric of meanings out of which we weave our lives. Chance is out of order, and even good luck is a slightly alarming idea for which we like to find personalised explanations.

Existentialism reverses these assumptions: chance is a burst of meaning into a world otherwise flattened out. The most outspoken defence of chance is made in Milan Kundera's novel *The Unbearable Lightness of Being*. 'Chance and change alone has a message for us.' For Kundera, everything else, all that is rationally predicable and habitual, is 'mute'. What we experience as 'chance' is anything that is not simply a *repetition* – if something recurs often and predictably, it becomes orderly, a structure in our lives, like the shopping trip or the journey to work. But then the occasion falls below the threshold of experience and meaning altogether. Like change, chance is the upsurge of the new, the unexpected, the singular happening. Compare two meetings. In the first, I see you every Wednesday at yoga classes; in the second, I run into you after years, on the platform at a big station. It is this second meeting which stays in the mind, as a unique occasion. The whole of my life passes in review around this sudden event. Could this be an important encounter? The chance meeting is news.

Every hour dozens of stray events pass by, just outside the range of attention. Chance is the name, for Kundera, and for Kierkegaard before him, for those unique events which catch the attention, and demand meaning.

see also...

Everyday; Meaning

Choice

Choice is a central theme in contemporary politics, economics and culture. We are often told that an increase in choice is a desirable goal of government policy or of commercial enterprise. We experience our own lives in terms of choices, or the denial of choices. If you try to define who you are, it is natural to think of the choices you have made, of relationships, of interests, careers, places, values. Who you are is what you choose, or would choose, if you were free. Existentialism is a philosophy of choice, and our tendency to define our lives in terms of our choices is partly a sign of the wider influence of this philosophy. But the existential thinkers focus as much on the painful aspects of choice as on the satisfaction. For example, in Sartre's novel *The Reprieve*, the hero Mathieu, alone, past the prime of youth, fearing the onset of the Second World War, looks at his life and sees a weird tyranny of choice. He surveys all the different choices he has made, and keeps having to make. Some of the choices are specific, like 'choosing his food and clothes', others are fleeting, such as choosing 'the trees and the houses he looked at'. But behind all the other choices, there is the bigger decision: 'choosing *himself* from day to day in the likeness of his thoughts'. Every second brings another choice, shall he turn his eye left or right, look up or down; every hour brings mundane decisions, what to have for breakfast; and every day poses again the question: who shall Mathieu choose to *be* now?

Of course, Mathieu is not free to start all over again every day. He has a job, he has beliefs which stay fixed. But no amount of constancy lifts from his shoulders the burden of further choices: he is choosing to stay as he is, just as much as he would be choosing to change his life. Sartre's hero has become acutely aware of the strange burden of making choices all life long: choice is one thing from which there is no escape.

see also...

Freedom; I

Christian Existentialism

The French philosopher Gabriel Marcel asserts that 'there is a Christian version of Existentialism'. He is not alone. Kierkegaard, Berdyaev, Jaspers, Tillich, Maritain, Auden: in different ways, and from different traditions, many thinkers have contributed to the project of a Christian Existentialism, which is important both to the history of Existentialism and to contemporary Christianity. In Marcel's famous declaration, Christian Existentialism is a way of being an Existentialist without having to abandon your faith. Marcel seems to be saying that nothing about Existentialism demands the relinquishing of faith and, as his tone implies, he is saying it in the face of objections from other Existentialists, notably Sartre, who held that the whole point of Existentialism was to be a philosophy of a godless world.

If Existentialists start from the experience of being, with nothing given, no fixed meanings, then surely they are making it easier to conceive of the world without reference to a deity? For many Existentialists, it *would* be a concession, even a defeat, to allow for the possibility of a Christian version.

Christian Existentialists nevertheless claim to find renewed religious hope precisely at the heart of this world emptied of the old categories and certainties. One, the Russian Berdyaev, even starts from the premise that 'In a certain sense we may say that Christianity is ending.' These are thinkers who aim to revive faith in new ways, or in an altered context: they are revolutionaries within their traditions: Russian Orthodox for Berdyaev, Protestant for Tillich and Auden, Catholic for Gabriel Marcel and Jacques Maritain. Marcel, for example, argues back to faith from the immediate experience of being. We live amidst 'presence', which is always 'a mystery'. I go for a walk down a lane and the trees surround me with their 'presence', the same presence to which religious worship testifies. Throughout our lives there runs 'the active recognition of something permanent', a recognition that comes before any doctrine or ideas.

see also...

Faith; Presence

Commitment

A woman is walking towards the entrance of a large, rather grand building. She pauses briefly at the threshold, and then pushes open the big door. She goes in. This might be just a mundane act: let's say she is a guest at a hotel, coming home for tea. But it might be more significant. Let's say it's an embassy, and she is about to unfurl a large banner which protests against the actions of that country's government. The pause becomes something different in these two cases. The guest is mechanically adjusting before entering the smart foyer. The protester is summoning up her spirits before she makes her gesture. The difference between the two people is one way of expressing the existential concept of 'commitment'.

There is a peculiar sense in which the two women are performing the same act, when each stretches out a hand to push the door. But for one it is an empty action; for the other it would be a defining moment where, in the words of Gabriel Marcel, an act 'commits my entire being as a person'. Her whole sense of herself in the world comes into play as she opens the door. Everything inside is lit up for her by her determined intention. She has become 'a person who is answerable': that is, she will stand by the actions which she is about to carry out, in the face of questions and challenges. Commitment is this experience of being 'answerable', or making oneself answerable, of taking it upon yourself to respond. There is nothing left over, in a moment when you are committed, in deed or in word: you cannot take refuge in the rest of your life, because your whole life is involved. You cannot, in commitment, say that you are normally not like this, that you are usually sensible and decent, say, like everyone else.

For Marcel, commitment can also be defined by the difference between a witness and an observer. The witness takes responsibility for what is seen, and reported; the observer remains detached. In commitment, we live as witnesses to the world.

see also...

Purpose; Sincerity

Community

We all belong to many communities; at work, in neighbourhoods, through family connections, religions, political beliefs, sexualities, musical tastes. Some of these communities are formally organized, others are more elusive; some seem to be matters of choice, others seem to enclose and define us in advance. No philosophy could be much help to us if it had nothing to say about the nature of community. It is true that Existentialism tends to start from the situation of the individual but, as many Existentialists have recognized, that situation cannot be understood apart from the ways it is shared with others.

Martin Buber looks from an existential point of view at 'the communal life of modern man'. Like other Existentialists, he sees many dangers and flaws in our communities, whether of work or identity, place or action. It can even seem as if some terrible force has 'destroyed almost every trace' of 'significant relation' in what pass for our communities. In other words, we belong passively, the communities seem fixed and mechanical. We are together with each other, but aren't really aware of each other as people. Our communities become like tube carriages in the rush hour, intensely shared spaces filled by co-existing strangers. In Sartre's version, the prisoner of war camp becomes the symbol of these false communities. The prisoners have 'a feeling that they were part of an organized society', which lifts from their shoulders the burden of thinking for themselves, or even being themselves. What then would a genuine community be like? For Buber the true 'structures of man's communal life' are those which 'draw their living quality from the power to enter into relation'. In other words, community is authentic when it seems to derive from each individual's actively forming connections, making and receiving contacts. A genuine community exists only insofar as these contacts renew themselves in each person's life. In some ways, this ideal of community reappears in the more optimistic versions of life on the internet, especially in the contrast between the communicative and the commercial internet.

> ## see also...
>
> *Dialogue; Relationship*

Consciousness

We usually talk of 'consciousness' as if it were inside the individual, a property of the person or of the mind. Think of some of the most common phrases. You recover consciousness after a bad fall: it is as if you had lost part of yourself and were now regaining it. Conversely, to lose consciousness suggests letting slip some part of yourself. If you think about 'consciousness-raising', it suggests adding more to this part of yourself. Existentialism has challenged these familiar ideas of consciousness in a number of ways.

The most fundamental challenge to ordinary assumptions, as often in the history of existential thought, comes from Sartre. He reverses the central and apparently most uncontentious aspect of ordinary views of consciousness, the assumption that it is an aspect of the individual alone. Sartre highly values the notion of individuality, yet he is always testing it and seeing its limits. So he insists that, contrary to common ideas, 'at the very heart of consciousness' there is 'a fundamental transcending connection with the Other'. Therefore, without any sense of this 'other', there can be no individual consciousness. Consciousness comes into being around a notion of relatedness: to be conscious means to connect 'I' and 'other'. The terms 'fundamental' and 'transcending' imply that this connection is not with any particular individual, it is more general. At the heart of consciousness is the abstracted notion of all others, of there being fellow beings in the world. Sartre might add that some have mistaken this general sense of the other for god: the word 'transcending' implies a kind of religious quality.

So in Sartre's terms, recovering consciousness means returning to a sense of the world, a world where 'I' exist always in relation to others. To lose consciousness would mean to sever all links both with the self and with the others. Most interestingly, to raise consciousness would involve a deepening of the connection with others, as well as an enriching of inner awareness.

see also...

Memory; Solipsism

Consequences

'You'll have to take the consequences …', we say, when we are warning someone against a certain action or utterance. For example, if you insist on saying what you really think, instead of being polite, at a crucial interview panel, then you must be aware of the consequences for your employment hopes. It's a slightly odd kind of warning, because the words don't actually tell the person not to do it, they point towards reasons against. 'Take the consequences' is another way of saying: you must realize what it is you are doing, you mustn't think you can disguise your choice or evade its nature. In the common phrase, consequences are both inevitable and negative, which is generally the case.

But now here is a crucial moment from the existential life of Sartre's fictional hero, Mathieu Delarue, in *The Age of Reason*. He has just had what seems to be a lucky escape. Having stolen some money, for various reasons, he seemed about to be exposed by the outraged victim, when mysteriously the cash is returned. Then Mathieu surveys the rest of his life and finds that this let-off is typical. For example, his lover Marcelle is pregnant, he has been searching for an abortionist, which is illegal and dangerous. Instead, she is going to get married. It turns out the same man, the sinister Daniel, is responsible both for the cash and for the marriage. There is, as Mathieu realizes, nothing well-intentioned about Daniel, and Mathieu protests in his presence: 'All I do, I do for *nothing*. It might be said that I am robbed of the consequences of my acts.' Without their consequences, our decisions and acts have no meaning. Freedom means nothing in a world where we never encounter the consequences of our choices.

In Sartre's existential usage, consequences are still fateful. Yet to avoid them all the time is not liberating but impoverishing. A life with no consequences might never have been lived: but how easy is it in a complex, modern society to encounter directly the consequences of an act, let alone a life?

see also...

Purpose; Responsibility

Courage

A man is getting into a carriage on an underground train. The space is already crowded and more people are pushing on behind him. He turns and wonders whether to get off, but he knows he will be late for work if he does. What is this man's state of mind? If he is worrying about the lateness, he could be impatient, annoyed, restless. If he is used to having his own space, he may be irritated or threatened. If he is afraid of confined spaces, even more if they are crowded, but still insists on continuing then he is in one of the states called courage.

This is a little experience of courage. But it shares with the big experiences the essential logic of courage: 'being in spite of'. In Tillich's major work, *The Courage To Be,* existential thought as a whole was reinvented using this idea of 'in spite of'. Many other moments in Existentialism contribute to a rich dialogue about the meaning of courage. For Tillich, courage is defined by whatever is being resisted: there is a courage in spite of death, and another courage in spite of anxiety. When Kierkegaard declares he possesses the courage to think a thought through, he is displaying the thinker's courage, to keep thinking in spite of the challenge and disturbance of the truth.

In modern times, Tillich believed, the main courage people need is the power to persist and continue, to affirm their own life, in the face of meaninglessness, the lack of any outside justification. Nor is courage just about sticking to the task: authentic courage means 'self-affirmation', the refusal to dismiss one's life in the face of guilt, in traditional terms, or meaninglessness, in more modern terms. It is only courage for as long as I refuse to come up with a consoling answer, to plead not guilty or to insist that I have found a meaning. The truest courage, then, is to affirm your life in the presence of its real limits, death or emptiness, the carriage from which no one ever gets off.

see also...

Existential Leap; Faith

Creativity

Existentialism does not encourage people to turn away from the actual fabric of their lives. On the contrary, there is often a deep regard for the texture of everyday experience. At the same time, Existentialism has been highly influential in making 'creativity' an important idea, or ideal, in contemporary culture. There is a potential conflict between this 'creativity' and the involvement in everydayness, the world as it greets us when we are living as we are. Doesn't creativity suggest something higher than, different from, ordinary experience, even a rejection of the limited realm of mundane reality?

If someone is 'creative', isn't he a touch above the ordinary? And isn't that why the claim of whole professions, like advertising, to define themselves as 'creative people' often annoys the rest of the world? In the most influential account of existential creativity, Paul Tillich seems to be denying this notion of special creative types. He argues that each person 'creates what he is' and that this 'creativity' is our freedom in action, since nothing fixes limits to it in advance. Everybody around you is by definition 'a creative person': there is no other way of becoming a person at all.

Yet Tillich also says the opposite: 'Not many people are creative.' Here he means that only a few are gifted with expressive talent, that can actually express the human predicament. This tension goes deep into the heart of Existentialism and particularly its influence in the wider culture. Seen in one way, existential principles make every person a creator; seen in another way, they point towards the special creativity of the great artist or thinker. Creativity is both unifying and divisive. This ambiguity has affected the practical impact of existential creativity in education. If the purpose of education is to nurture creativity, does that mean it should primarily support every child in making a world, or is the aim to foster specific and special talents for expression? Can the conflict be reconciled? The answer to these educational questions is probably critical for the future influence and shape of Existentialism.

see also...

Becoming; Lack

Cynicism

A government spokesperson announces that the economy is showing signs of recovery, as a result of their policies. A scientist is interviewed and declares that the latest discovery will definitely be both safe and beneficial. The chances are that you don't believe them: at best, you suspend your doubts, at worst you give another gloomy shrug and get on with your life. Authority is no longer readily trusted: are we all becoming cynical then? And is that the choice, either believe what we are told, or become a cynic?

Existentialism is important partly because it seeks alternatives beyond this choice we so often face, between an impossible trust in authority and a seemingly limitless cynicism. Nietzsche put the question at the end of the nineteenth century: 'Before one seeks men one must have found the lantern. Will it have to be the lantern of the cynic?' What he meant was that future ages would not settle for the old values and beliefs: there would be a new demand for light to be shone into all the dark places, all the hidden motives, the suppressed facts. Would the result have to be cynicism? Iris Murdoch carried this story forward, when she described the characters from Sartre's novels of the 1940s as 'people from after the deluge'. For these characters, and for the rest of us too, the established values have been lost. No-one, or hardly anyone, automatically trusts the old authorities. Yet, Murdoch says, these modern people show neither 'Satanism [n]or … cynicism'. They face the world as it is, questioning, sceptical but not cynical. They seek for ways to disbelieve the official line, without being trapped into endless disbelief of all ideals and ideas. Murdoch adds, for herself, that 'Cynical frivolity is the reaction of those who are still under the sway of the morality which they deny.' Only someone who feels he ought to believe this expert, or accept that rule, will feel like a rebellious cynic when he doesn't comply. Instead you can pick up the lantern, and go looking for the truth.

see also...

Honesty; Value

Darwin, Charles

Charles Darwin (1809–82) established the scientific theory of evolution, notably through his most famous book *The Origin of Species by Means of Natural Selection* (1859). At the centre of Darwin's thought is the term 'existence': evolution is driven onward by a perpetual 'Struggle For Existence'. Therefore Darwin's work was a major factor in promoting the defining term of Existentialism, the philosophy which starts its account of the world, and particularly the human world, from the basic fact of existence, which comes before any other facts. But Darwin also has a deeper affinity with Existentialism.

The core of Darwin's theory is his explanation of 'how species arise in nature'. In the biblical view of creation, every species has a fixed nature: each acts 'after its kind', and the same is true of human beings. Darwin denies that there are any fixed 'kinds': he sees species as constantly changing entities, whose boundaries are often ambiguous. In Darwin's view, the natural world is made up of 'organic beings', each committed to a struggle for existence by the scarcity of resources, food and space. In that struggle, some individuals will turn out to have 'advantages', which will allow the favoured ones to survive and breed, passing on their characteristics to their offspring. Over time, a whole species will be transformed as those who lack the advantages fail to survive and reproduce. Over a long period, these changes produce the beginnings of a new species. This theory, Natural Selection, is very compatible with both the terms and the principles of Existentialism, though not all individual Existentialists have adopted it. The world is seen in terms of changing beings, engaged in an active process, seeking to root themselves more firmly in existence, and involved in 'infinitely complex relations' with all other organic beings. Darwin gives scientific credibility to the existential idea of beings who make themselves what they are, beings who have no eternal nature. The continued authority of evolutionary theory indicates that Existentialism has a major part to play in the new century.

see also...

Existence; Superman

Decision

I decide to break off a relationship. If it's a real decision, then the moment becomes a gap in time, a gap across which there is no passing back. In a decision, I exert my will to the uttermost, but with a certain paradoxical effect: that I am prevented from exerting my will on another occasion as freely in the opposite direction. In other words, in a true decision, my present will is so strong that it takes away some of the scope from my will in the future. If I then try to re-start the relationship, it turns out not to have been a real moment of decision at all. Yet there is another odd feature of decision. I have just made a big decision: to leave my job, say. Out I go, and in the coffee bar round the corner I am asked to decide between four sizes of coffee cup and ten kinds of froth. That decision too is irreversible: once I have paid and drunk, I can't have the choice back again.

Decisions belong to the existential problem of freedom in time. Simone de Beauvoir dramatizes the paradoxes of decision with tragic vividness: 'Go on, go on, decide. Every beat of my heart casts into the world a decision from which there is no recall.' Recall is an illusion: decisions are irrevocable, if they are real decisions. This irrevocability is the difference between just doing something and really having decided to do it. Yet though true decisions may be irreversible, they do not prevent the next decision from coming along immediately: 'every beat of my heart' faces me with another.

From de Beauvoir's staggering insight emerges a general irony. The one decision it seems we cannot make is the decision to face no more decisions: 'Go on, go on.' Every moment presents new possibilities of deciding, and we cannot choose to renounce these possibilities as long as we remain in time. Decisions alter everything, yet in another way they leave everything unchanged: 'Refuse to exist: I exist. Decide to exist: I exist. Refuse. Decide. I exist.'

see also...

Anguish; Choice

Derrida, Jacques

Born in French Algeria in 1930, Jacques Derrida has become the leading French exponent of the philosophical and literary movement called deconstruction. But he is also in many ways a leading reinterpreter of Existentialism. His influence on modern literature and philosophy stems from *Of Grammatology* (1967) and *Dissemination* (1972). Existential themes and texts have been increasingly central as Derrida has sought to redefine his thinking. Major examples include: *Of Spirit: Heidegger and The Question* (1987), *Cinders* (1987) and *The Gift of Death* (1992). Throughout his work, Derrida returns to reassess the major existential thinkers, notably Kierkegaard, Nietzsche and Heidegger. Increasingly, he seeks to place their ideas in relation to the darkest scenes of the twentieth century, including the Holocaust itself.

In *The Gift of Death*, Derrida re-examines the relationship between language and freedom as understood by Kierkegaard and other Existentialists. For Derrida, each of us retains an 'absolute singularity', and yet when I speak I must use words that belong to others before they come to me. Therefore, argues Derrida, we face a contradiction between our sense of ourselves as distinct and autonomous, and our experience of language. The moment you start to argue about your individuality in words, you are compromising it. Derrida turns this idea back upon the work of Kierkegaard and others, in celebration and renewed inquiry.

In *Cinders*, Derrida assembles a series of reflections and quotations, all connected to the phrase 'Cinders there are'. He uses this phrase to recreate the existential question of existence and meaning. What does it mean for cinders to exist? By implication, Derrida is exploring what the twentieth century has done to the problem of being. He tries to define the existence of the cinder as, for example, 'the difference between what remains and what is'. A cinder belongs neither to the past nor to the present. Through this subtle metaphor, Derrida asks us to think again about existence and time.

see also...

Responsibility; Sacrifice

Dialogue

You only need turn on the news to become aware of the possibility of endless dialogue. On any given day, there is bound to be an announcement that one or another dialogue is to continue, despite there being little prospect for an early resolution. These potentially endless dialogues arise when countries are on the verge of war, when wars are coming to an end, when states are breaking up or being founded, when hostages are taken or prisoners will be released. Though experts and participants always remind us that the issues are complex, and that there are no simple answers, we need no such education. We all know that the talks will go on through the night, over the weekend, at a secret location, with a new chairman, and so on. Endless dialogue is a fact of modern life: there is only one thing worse, it seems, and that is the sudden breakdown of these dialogues. There will follow an interlude of violence, before the talking must start again.

Throughout the world, as we hear its news, the alternatives appear to be immediate violence or endless dialogue. In many ways, these alternatives reflect the world as conceived by Existentialism. One of the most touching examples is the praise of the ancient Greek philosopher Socrates, given by Martin Buber. Socrates has come down to us as the main speaker in Plato's philosophical dialogues. He was put to death by the authorities for subversion: asking too many awkward questions. Buber celebrates Socrates as 'the I of endless dialogue': he never gives up on the dialogue, he always responds to the other side. Buber sees Socrates followed by 'the air of dialogue' even in front of his hostile judges and finally at 'the last hour in prison'. You could be cynical and say: all that talking did no good in the end. Or you could say that the ideal of dialogue stayed faithful to itself, in the face of oppression. Endless dialogue represents what Karl Jaspers called 'utter openness', an unvanquished patience with the being of others.

see also...

Address; Others

Earth

We have got used to the image of the earth seen from space: earthrise, the blue and white globe rising above the horizon of the moon, photographed by US astronauts. This image has helped to create the environmental movement which will be one of the main legacies of the twentieth century. One of the founding ideas of this environmental movement is that human life isn't separable from the earth as a whole; we cannot take humanity seriously without taking the earth equally seriously. In many ways, Existentialism helped prepare the context in which the image of the globe became so significant.

Nietzsche, through Zarathustra, exhorted us to 'remain faithful to the earth'. Traditional religions, Nietzsche believed, offered the false hope of a life beyond the confines of the earth, an other-worldly refuge. For Zarathustra, faith should not seek to reach beyond the earth; on the contrary, faith should attach us ever more securely to the planet we actually inhabit, here and now. We must not look, Zarathustra warns, for meaning outside the earth; instead, our aim should be to give new meaning to the earth. As we enrich our own being, developing the possibilities of humanity, we will also deepen our bond to the earth. The human relationship to the earth will grow as human life advances, beyond its own confines. Here, potentially, is an alternative criterion of progress: instead of technological advance, or economic expansion, the criterion of progress could be 'the meaning of the earth'.

The earth becomes part of the human condition; in existential terms, you cannot begin by defining humanity and then place your fixed human beings on the planet. Instead, the search for the meaning of human existence will go hand in hand with a drive to enrich our sense of the earth. For the political philosopher Hannah Arendt, human life was unthinkable without certain biological processes, like birth and death, and also without 'the earth'. Is that why the main image from the space age is not the moon or the stars, but the old earth?

see also...

Meaning; World

Emotion

What is emotion? What is meant by saying 'I am angry' or 'I am in love'? Often these statements of feeling are seen as referring to a strange biochemical reality or a biological world of instincts and drives. Existentialism certainly does not deny the connections between emotion and the body. But within existential thinking there is a consistent rejection of reducing emotion to pure biology or chemistry. Instead, emotion is seen as an aspect of our human consciousness of the world. Imagine you are going to a party, and you are just getting out of the car outside. You look out at the lights flickering through the windows, and you hear the voices and music. It all seems too loud, too crowded, altogether too much. That is a perception of the outside world, including a lot of straightforward facts. But it is also one of the ways in which you can tell how you feel: in this case, the world comes back to you coloured by irritable tiredness, perhaps boredom, maybe a hint of fear. Now by contrast take the occasion where you see the same things and move forward with enthusiastic eagerness to join in.

The world comes back to you in a way which tells you of your feelings of happy anticipation.

These examples reflect Iris Murdoch's view that, within Existentialism, 'Emotion is primarily consciousness of the world as qualified in a certain way.' You become aware of how you feel not by introspection but by noticing the colouring of your experience. In other words, emotion is an aspect of our human way of being in the world. Therefore, whatever the ingredients mixed in the nervous system, emotion affects us as an organic aspect of our whole being.

We cannot abstract this or that feeling from the occasion or the story we are living. In *The Outsider*, Camus' hero Mersault is repeatedly accused of failing to display correct emotions. This forms part of his prosecution for murder: to regulate emotion externally is to deny its true nature, and so to suppress being in favour of artificial categories. The outcome is injustice.

see also...

Fear; Love

Equipment

The weather forecast is on TV: on the map are little arrows which tell me which way the wind is blowing tomorrow. I notice the patterns, but I don't really take in the information. Now I am outside, and the wind is blowing, quite gently: I am aware ot the sensation, but only vaguely. But in the next scene, I am a farmer, going out into the fields to decide whether it's harvest time. The wind is blowing and this time I notice it in a different way: I know as I feel the sensation that it's a south wind, that it means the weather will be fine, that I should go and get the harvester ready. For the TV watcher, the arrows are patterns that could be read as signs if he needed to know about the wind. For the walker, the wind is just a light touch. For the farmer, the wind is something he is using: he is using it as a sign of the weather, and that's because he has a purpose. In the context of that purpose, the wind is made into what Heidegger calls 'equipment', for signs are just a particular type of equipment.

Anything becomes 'equipment' if we encounter it in terms of its usefulness to us. The obvious examples, of course, would be tools, hammers or computers. But 'equipment' is, as the south wind and the farmer suggests, a wider concept than these obvious tools. When we turn anything into a sign, and read it from the point of view of some project of our own, then that sign is also a kind of equipment. The farmer is using the wind just as much as he is going to use his harvester. Both are a form of equipment, for him.

When we encounter things as equipment, we are aware of them in a highlighted way. Moreover, we are aware of them in relation to each other: the south wind and the harvester both belong to the world in terms of the farmer's 'involvement', his concern to get something done.

see also...

Objects; Purpose

Essence

In all its forms, Existentialism is committed to resisting any idea that some essential nature explains the way individuals and societies *act*, and do not act. There is, for Existentialists, no human essence which dictates what we become, or how we live. Often, especially faced with some terrible event, commentators start talking about human nature, the dark side of human beings or the fear of the unknown or the natural hostility to foreigners. Or experts will talk about the essential nature of, say, the Balkans, or of Ireland, as if there were some unchanging and unchangeable force governing people and their actions. From the perspective of Existentialism, Simone de Beauvoir denounces this as a phoney explanation: 'it is not a mysterious essence that compels men and women to act in good or in bad faith, it is their situation that inclines them more or less towards the search for truth'. That is, people find themselves in situations that do indeed shape their choices; but there is no eternal essence at work, only concrete circumstances that we could change.

If there is no grand human nature, there can also be no lesser essences, no essence of manhood or womanliness, no timeless Jewish essence or Englishness. In the words of de Beauvoir, there are no 'unchangeably fixed entities' which make us what we are. Society may impose stereotypes, but they can be resisted or changed. De Beauvoir develops the existential case against 'essences' into a criticism of 'femininity' as the most widespread dogma of essential character. 'Although some women try zealously to incarnate this essence', she declares with some sarcasm, it remains 'unpatentable', that is, no one is ever going to bottle it, whatever the perfume ads may say. There are different bodies and sexual drives, but de Beauvoir in the 1940s speaks for the most forward-looking currents in Existentialism when she argues that 'sexuality has never seemed to us to define a destiny'. Sexuality has no fixed meaning or consequence. In a just society, each woman would be free to define, or disregard, 'the concept of femininity' in her own terms – and each man might re-make the concept of masculinity.

see also...

Existence; Humanity

Ethics

'It is no good arguing with ethics …'. This statement, by Kierkegaard, is one of the most memorable in Existentialism. It sounds as if he means that we never have any alternative to following the moral rules, that the laws of right and wrong are as fixed now as they seemed to be in childhood: don't pull his hair; put that back, it belongs to someone else. Kierkegaard *is* saying that the moral rules are hard to bend, but he is also saying something more subversive, that there is something arbitrary about ethics, the accepted definitions of good and bad. You cannot argue because these judgements are norms which put themselves above discussion: they are as they are, that's all. So indeed, from the perspective of a child, we are often told that arguing back makes the offence worse.

Certainly for Kierkegaard, and other Existentialists, it isn't easy to set aside the normal judgements. As Kierkegaard also says, 'the ethical is the universal'. If a value is truly ethical, then it applies to all times and places. If it's wrong to steal, then that's true everywhere. The rules are the rules, but the world is the world,

and in between there are all sorts of gaps, some small, others large. These gaps separate the general, where ethics rules, from the particular. True, most of the time the particular fits snugly enough inside the general categories, so that we don't notice the gaps. But there is always the potential for trouble. In extreme cases we have what Kierkegaard calls 'the teleological suspension of the ethical'. Teleology is about final things, ultimate purposes. In extreme cases, such ultimate purposes overrule the ethical altogether. Then the act remains ethically wrong, but the judgement is simply irrelevant. A mother steals to save a child: but ethics can cope, because the saving theft is too obviously good in some wider sense. The gap can be closed with thought. But when Abraham plans to murder Isaac at God's will, the act remains murder, in intention: and yet it is redeemed by its ultimate meaning, pure resignation in absolute faith. Ethics is surpassed.

see also...

Sacrifice; Tragedy

Everyday

It is natural to assume that if philosophy is about deep questions, then philosophers cannot be interested in ordinary, everyday life. That is one reason for all the stereotypes of absent-minded intellectuals, crashing down the stairs as they ponder the destiny of the universe. Existentialism certainly demands an engagement with big issues, the meaning of life, the value of action, the nature of freedom. But Existentialists have not seen any contradiction between such 'deep' interests and the appeal of everyday life.

Nietzsche is certainly not a down-to-earth character in the usual sense. He is given to paradoxes and extreme statements. Yet one of his favoured voices, a character called 'The Wanderer', is made to condemn Western thinking for 'being unknowledgeable in the smallest and most everyday things'. According to this wise speaker, when people fail to 'keep an eye' on these everyday things, then they lose their way in the world. As a result life then appears to be a mere ordeal, without meaning or purpose. If we want to discover meaning in life, we should not begin by scanning the horizon, or look for big concepts to rescue us. Instead, we should 'become good neighbours to the closest things'. When people find life blank or pointless, they tend to look for big concepts to rescue them: 'Progress' or 'God', say, or 'History' or 'the Nation' or even 'Truth'. They are looking in exactly the wrong direction. There is more support to be found in the humble things that fill our everyday gaze when we get up in the morning. If you set off in pursuit of 'meaning' in the abstract, you are just chasing what Nietzsche calls 'clouds and monsters of the night'. But if you really try to *notice* the movement of those curtains in the breeze, or the hum of the coffee machine, then you will begin to awaken to the texture of life. That is why Heidegger too refused to dismiss 'average everydayness', however dull and dimmed, since it still contains the beginnings of pathways to new illumination.

see also...

Appearances; Reality

Existence

What is existence? To be gripped by this question is to become drawn towards Existentialism. But the particular way in which Existentialists have found the question of existence gripping concerns human beings. The big question is what existence means for human beings. To apply the terms of Heidegger, Existentialism evolves as an inquiry into 'man's being'. This being has no fixed definition, except that its 'essence' cannot be found apart, but 'lies in its existence'. Why does this definition matter so much?

If human beings have an essence which can be separated from their existence, then it makes sense to talk about a fixed human nature. For example, it might be an essential characteristic of humanity to defend territory, or to need love. The same would apply to individuals. If there is an individual essence that stands apart from existence, then you can talk about someone having unalterable qualities that define their character. She is essentially a nervous person, nothing caused it and nothing is going to change it. He is an aggressive character, and that's

how it is. Heidegger accepts that we have, of course, got our characteristics. But he denies these are 'properties' of 'man's being', either collectively or individually. What that means is that human nature gets defined in the process of being expressed. If people are in need of love, in this situation, then that is how 'man's being' has expressed itself here and now. If a woman is nervous, that is how 'man's being' expresses itself in her life, as it is lived in this world which surrounds her. This need and nervousness are not fixed properties, they express being as it unfolds, they are possible 'ways for it to be'. Existence is a process in which being finds itself, and nothing can be said of human life outside that process.

see also...

Being; Darwin

Existential Deviation

Let's say you are being bullied at work. It seems you just can't do anything right. Everywhere you go, you are told of something else you did wrong, though you know it's not fair. You leave, you go home and gradually the tainted feeling fades. But now imagine that the feeling does not go away: those disapproving voices won't stop. Even when you aren't there, your life becomes defined by their objections to you. Eventually, you can't see yourself independently of all that abuse.

In that case, your life has been taken out of your hands, you are living from an alien and negative point of view. The outcome is a small-scale example of what the African Existentialist Frantz Fanon termed 'existential deviation'. You are pushed sideways whenever you try to look at yourself in your own way: it is as if you can't get direct access to your own being. In his major work, *Black Skin, White Masks*, Fanon gave an existential account of the impact of racist colonialism on the colonized. Under colonization, the struggle to create yourself freely is doubly difficult. You have to begin from the hostile gaze which is always directed at you. As Fanon says, the racist society greeted his appearance by exclaiming over and over: 'Look, a negro!'. He was always required to overcome not just the general predicament of humanity, the absence of a given identity; he was faced immediately by an alien and hostile definition: 'here I was called on for more'. In the words of Lewis Gordon, a contemporary African-American Existentialist, Fanon had to achieve 'liberation from being determined by another', and determined in the negative.

Ironically, this added dimension of existential struggle makes the nature of freedom even clearer. By freedom, Fanon meant the ending of social and political barriers, physical and economic captivity, but he also meant liberation from the other's distorting consciousness. By seeking to inflict an 'existential deviation' on the oppressed, the oppressor claimed for himself a false position in the world, the god-like position from which others are defined as if by right.

see also...

Other; Shame

Existential Leap

'Ulster takes leap of faith': that was the headline which greeted news of an historic agreement in the political history of Northern Ireland. The same headline could as readily have applied to South Africa when a deal was reached between Nelson Mandela and the previous ruling powers, or to the Middle East, or any other area where a difficult resolution is being undertaken. The 'leap of faith' is one of the most widely influential concepts developed within the traditions of Existentialism. Its original context is personal faith, and that remains at the heart of the 'existential leap'.

The metaphor of leaping belongs to a wider rejection by Existentialists of smoothness and easy links. The leap is the act, inner or outer, by which the world is re-made. In the leap, we overcome the limits of the way things are, and particularly the limits as endorsed by reason. Kierkegaard gives one of the most important images of the existential leap when he tries to describe true faith. He says that such faith is beyond him, in practice; he can only strive to grasp it in metaphors and by stretching his

ideas. I have faith, he asserts, if 'I am able to make from the springboard the great leap whereby I pass into infinity'. At no point can we pass by accumulation from the finite to infinity: the required movement is therefore a leap. As seekers of faith, each of us lives like 'a tight-rope-dancer', poised to try a new and more dangerous leap. The true leap of faith is like an impossible perfection in dance, it means 'to leap into a definite posture in such a way that there is not a second in which he is grasping after the posture'. You cannot evolve faith: it has to be there suddenly, all in one go. Yet you must prepare yourself continuously, and you can only achieve faith by an act of your own will.

Nietzsche makes his voice Zarathustra define 'man' as 'a rope over an abyss'. We need to leap and dance upon this rope, if we are to change.

see also...

Justification; Reasons

Existential Position

We tend to think of ourselves and others as having a certain temperament. I tend to be optimistic, she is usually a pessimist. Existential thought is unfriendly towards this way of thinking, because it makes character sound fixed, as if inside each person there is a pre-ordained mechanism. On the other hand, Existentialism does recognize that there is a consistency to many lives. How then can there be a vocabulary for talking about continuity of character and experience which does not pin each person down and make every action the outer effect of an inner principle which can never alter?

One important idea is the 'existential position', used to great effect in the therapeutic theories of R D Laing. Laing defines 'existential position' as 'the person's experience of his world and of himself'. In Laing's approach, it was the role of the therapist to achieve 'an understanding of the patient's existential position'. This meant something very different from classifying the person's temperament or condition. The existential position makes sense only from inside, from the viewpoint of the person in question. Laing gives as an example a patient who says he is made of glass and is terrified of being shattered. Laing recognizes that there is a kind of appalling truth to this vision: 'We may suppose that precisely as such he experiences himself.' The question then is how it came about that a person could experience himself, and his world, in such a way, and what might alter the experience. But everyone has such a position, at any given time and often over long periods of time. Listen to a person's favourite catchphrase: 'quite frankly', says the person whose existential position is that of being distrusted. 'I can't blame you' recurs as a phrase in the life of the person whose existential position is that of constant betrayal and disappointment. 'In an ideal world' says the person whose existential position is a feeling of unyielding hardness to the world. 'I can't help being a bit concerned' speaks of a fear of being drowned in a sea of unending concerns.

see also...

I; *Therapy*

Faith

Existentialism finds faith hard to comprehend. So many questions need to be asked, so many choices have to be made, every day, every hour: how is a stable and deep faith possible? Much existential thought *has* cast doubt upon established creeds or values, whether religious, political or moral. Yet Existentialists have also distinguished between faith as a way of fitting in, being one of the community, and faith as an individual achievement. This personal faith is often highly valued by Existentialists, and their ideas have influenced modern developments in religion and beyond.

A moving existential account of faith is given by Søren Kierkegaard in his re-telling of the story of Abraham and Isaac. Abraham has been promised a son by God; now he is old, his wife Sarah is old, and no son has been born. Others mock his hopes, but Abraham will not deny the promise: 'By faith Abraham went out from the land of his fathers, and became a sojourner in the land of promise.' In other words, Abraham became an outsider, he held to a belief that all around him found absurd. Existentialism values faith which is able to flourish in exile. Kierkegaard also values Abraham's faith because it seeks fulfilment here on earth: 'But Abraham believed precisely for this life'. Then comes the second stage. The son is born, grows up and suddenly the angel asks Abraham to sacrifice his dearest Isaac. Kierkegaard can find no way of understanding Abraham's willingness to perform the act, right up to the point where the angel returns and releases Isaac: 'Abraham I cannot understand, in a certain sense there is nothing I can learn from him but astonishment.' Kierkegaard calls Abraham a 'knight of faith', and admits that he has never actually come across such a person. Existentialism is often negative, and sometimes seems to deny all hope of belief or stable values. But there is also space for an ideal of faith, whether religious, political or ethical, an ideal of personal commitment and an ability to live 'in the land of promise' and transcend 'the land of the fathers'.

see also...

Absurd; Christian Existentialism

Fall

Why is falling a common nightmare? Why do so many people share this dream experience of the sudden drop, the endless descent? Are we all afraid of falling, is this some universal fear? According to Existentialism, this falling which haunts so many dreams isn't about fear, though it looks fearful. The philosophical novelist Milan Kundera calls the falling dream 'vertigo' and then insists it is 'something other than the fear of falling'. For Kundera, the fall is our response to the inviting call of 'the emptiness below', the lure of non-being.

In Heidegger's more abstract terms, the falling sensation which surfaces most vividly in such dreams is above all about moving away, drifting off. We don't fall towards anything, we fall away from everything. That is probably why we wake up before we hit the ground: there is no ground to hit. For Heidegger, this falling feeling is an expression of fundamental anxiety, the recoil from the world and our own participation in that world. Fear, says Heidegger, shrinks back from something, and seeks safety somewhere else. Anxiety falls away from everything, and so there is nothing left for it to seek. Falling is the shadow of true freedom. Falling, we surrender ourselves, and lose everything; in true freedom, we become ourselves in the midst of everything.

Yet as Kundera recognizes, the harder you try to climb, the more alluring the fall can sound. Within the anxiety, there may be a desire: to stop the effort of becoming a person in the world. Imagine if being yourself was as easy as falling through space. The dream is, therefore, evidence that Existentialism is on to something when it talks of the active engagement required to live a life. This is the dream against which our anxiety defends us.

Others have seized the falling dream differently. For Nietzsche, there is such a thing as the deliberate and active fall: 'Thus Zarathustra began to go under.' In the story of Zarathustra, the freedom of falling meets with the exertion of the will: this is a free fall towards knowledge.

see also...

Anxiety; World

Fanon, Frantz

Frantz Fanon (1925–61) was a leading intellectual influence on anti-colonial thought and politics. Born in the French Antilles, Fanon drew upon a wide range of ideas, including the psychoanalytic theories he encountered while qualifying and working as a psychiatrist. He also developed his ideas in a complex dialogue with European Existentialism, notably the work of Sartre. Fanon's major works were composed in French and widely translated throughout the world. They include *Black Skin, White Masks* (1952) and *The Wretched of the Earth* (1961).

In his Preface to *The Wretched of the Earth*, Sartre declared that here the world of the colonies and former colonies 'finds itself and speaks to itself'. For Sartre, Fanon represented a new voice, a new self-consciousness in the history of human self-creation. The Afro-American existential philosopher Paget Henry saw in Fanon the distinctive concern with 'liberation from being defined by the Other'. The affirmative side of this liberation is summed up by Robert Birt as bringing to birth 'a new humanity'. For such thinkers, Fanon has interwoven the themes of

Existentialism and anti-imperialism. His work redefines the problems of self-creation and the Other from the perspective of those searching for freedom in the face of colonial oppression. Fanon himself came to play a practical role in the post-colonial politics of Algeria.

Fanon's writing is distinguished by its intense commitment. Yet he never offers easy answers, and at the heart of his work is a sense of inquiry. As he says in *Black Skin, White Masks*, he will give the reader no 'timeless truths'. In the same work, he sees the predicament of the colonized as being made 'always contingent', defined by reference to the colonialist, the Other. The colonized peoples are made into 'comparison'. In their situation, the struggle for political freedom is also a means towards existential liberation, the overthrowing of this distorting relationship. In *The Wretched of the Earth*, Fanon calls, in existential terms, for a new decision.

see also...
Existential Deviation; Revolution

Fascism

Fascism is one of the terrifying facts of mid-twentieth century history. It is a fact which has a defining importance for Existentialism too, as a development always concerned to respond to the challenge of the modern. In some cases, Existentialism can be seen as compromised in its connection with fascism, most notoriously in the life of Martin Heidegger. But even then, Heidegger's ideas continued to influence many thinkers on the anti-fascist side. In the thought of Sartre and de Beauvoir, particularly, Existentialism confronted fascism as the defining *threat* of modern times. In their work, fascism is the extreme example of many different arguments.

In their interpretations of fascism, Sartre and de Beauvoir relentlessly followed through the nature of existential philosophy. The most overwhelming statement on fascism is given to a resistance leader by de Beauvoir: 'if Fascism were to triumph, that's just what would happen. There would be no more human beings …'. This sounds a strange and alarming conclusion. Fascism, with its genocidal motives and its violent authoritarianism, obviously threatens many human values. But for de Beauvoir, if fascism were to establish itself, human beings themselves would cease. This argument is possible because of the idea that humanity is not a fixed entity, but a process of expression and development. If that process can be created, then it can also be destroyed. Fascism is the force which, in modern times, is attempting to annihilate the process by which man's being creates itself in the world. Freedom is the key. There can be no human beings in the total absence of freedom, because it is part of the meaning of the 'human' to confront the world through its own freedom. If that experience is impossible, then what we mean by human beings will be excluded.

In a famous and controversial statement, Sartre perhaps simplified this idea as part of an account of 'Existentialism and Humanism'. He considered what would happen if fascism were ever the winner, and announced that in the event 'Fascism will then be the human reality, so much the worse for us.'

see also...

Humanity; Superman

Fear

Fear is a feeling of being trapped. If I am afraid of someone, then at the thought of him my world seems to change. His presence breaks in upon my world, and I find myself sharing the space with him. As a result, I seem to have less room than before, and I am also busy thinking of ways to escape. My problem will be that I can only get away from him by also leaving behind my world, as it used to be. The stronger the fear, the more insistent becomes this threatening presence inside my world. In this sense, fear can be seen as one opposite of love: it is a negative equivalent to the positive sharing of a world that comes about through love.

It is in Kierkegaard that the discussion of fear and love is richest. But the most compelling existential account of fear itself comes from Heidegger. In his work, fear is represented by a feeling that 'it is coming close'. There are lots of threatening things. Most of the time, we live without feeling the threat directly. But fear is the feeling that a potential threat has broken in: 'In fearing as such, what we have thus characterized as threatening is freed and allowed to matter to us.' The world is full of things, events and people which are, or may be, threats to me. But most of the time the vast majority are simply beyond my scope of concern. These things do not matter to me, although if they did I would be afraid of them. That is how I live with all kinds of news and information, potential health risks which I am not avoiding, or political terrors that lie in wait among every day's headlines. Fear does not create the threat, but it is the feeling of that state of mind in which a particular threat matters to me. Once it has mattered, strangely, we find difficulty ever recalling how this threat was not fearful. Fear is a source of both insight and illusion: it makes things matter.

see also...

Insecurity; Lack

47

Freedom

Almost every political party claims to be in favour of 'freedom'. In most moral or social debates, to show that an action will preserve or enhance 'freedom' is a strong argument. But 'freedom' means so many different things, from unhampered economic activity to the right to publish controversial ideas, from sexual choice to open information. In the end, it seems as if the word 'freedom' has lost its meaning, or could mean almost anything. Yet Existentialism can make the idea of 'freedom' both urgent and challenging for us.

In Sartre's *The Age of Reason*, a man and a woman are arguing. They are lovers, and she is pregnant. Decisions are approaching. The woman, Marcelle, declares angrily that 'You want to be free. Absolutely free. It's your vice.' The man, Mathieu, replies edgily: 'What else can a man do?' Here is the paradox of existential freedom in a nutshell: the one choice people cannot make is the choice to deny their own freedom. He goes on to add that everyone is in the same boat, compelled to be free, but many simply haven't woken up to this predicament. Such freedom is not a luxury, it is not even a right: it is an inevitability. In the words of Iris Murdoch, 'We are condemned to be free.'

In some ways, this is a very severe view of freedom. The soldier is ordered to pull the trigger. He is at the bottom of an immense system of command and control. Anyway, he has been fed an endless pack of lies by the powers that be, so that he sees the victim as a terrible threat to civilization. Surely, such a soldier can argue that he was not making a free choice when he fired the shot? In existential terms, as understood by Sartre and Murdoch, the soldier could never shrug off from his shoulders the burden of responsibility: he always remains free, however cramped the circumstances. Such freedom, though, is a question, and not an answer: as Marcelle angrily reflects later, 'Freedom didn't help a person to live.'

see also...

Action; Decision

God

Probably the most notorious statement in the history of Existentialism is 'God is dead!', the announcement relayed by Nietzsche's prophetic voice, Zarathustra. But what does it mean to say that God is dead? For one thing, it must mean that there was a living presence, so this can't be an example of simple atheism in the sense of the absolute and unconditional denial of the deity. For another thing, the death of gods is a central event in many world mythologies, including the Greek and Egyptian legends. In fact, what Zarathustra says is that there is nothing in the least surprising about this news. He has just met an isolated hermit in the forest, and now he reflects: 'Could it be possible? This old man in the forest has not yet heard anything of this, that God is dead!' The shock is that anyone could be unaware of the death, which has been foreshadowed by thousands of mythical narratives and, in Zarathustra's terms, experienced by millions of people.

The hermit described a life still based upon God's presence. Every action is performed in praise of the deity. So if God is dead, then there is nothing being addressed by all these actions or words: the hermit is dancing in a void, under the illusion of having an approving audience. But it's not just saints who have lost their witness: sinners have also lost their God: 'but God died, and these sinners died with him.' They died *as* sinners, for their acts could no longer confer on them any such identity. The world has lost the centre from which all categories took their resonance. Now there are no saints and no sinners.

Instead there are questions, and the key question, as Karl Jaspers says picking up Nietzsche's story, is now 'what will become of man'. Jaspers wrote as one sympathetic to religion, and he sees the death of God as an 'historical situation' through which humanity must pass, on the way to a different meaning. Nietzsche's Zarathustra had defined the question to which many then sought their own answers.

see also...

Atheism; Presence

Heidegger, Martin

The German philosopher Martin Heidegger (1889–1976) is the most controversial figure in the entire history of Existentialism. In *Being and Time* (1927) he produced the single most influential and original work of existential thought. This book was, in fact, only one part of a larger projected project but even in this supposedly incomplete form it reshaped the agenda of Existentialism and transformed the landscape for subsequent thinkers like Sartre, de Beauvoir, Murdoch, Camus and Laing. Heidegger wrote *Being and Time* from 1923–7. Previously known as a Catholic philosopher, he broke out of this theological tradition, and came under the influence particularly of Edmund Husserl, who was developing an approach known as 'phenomenology', the science of 'the thing'. Heidegger begins his own philosophy by posing the 'question of being', which he claims has been passed over in the West since very early Greek thought. According to Sartre, in *Being and Nothingness*, Heidegger created space for new advances by proceeding in 'his abrupt, rather barbaric fashion' to give new definitions of ancient terms. For Sartre, the most important terms were 'world' 'being-in' and 'being'. Heidegger redefined philosophy as the inquiry into 'dasein', man's existence, literally the 'being-there' of man. He turned thought back upon itself, proclaiming that 'we are ourselves the entities to be analysed'.

Heidegger shows us humanity 'thrown' into the 'world'. He explores the moods of our understanding. He redefines what it means to be 'authentic'. Heidegger pursued this inquiry in other works, notably 'What is Metaphysics?' (1929). Yet in 1933 this liberating influence, for many, showed himself an enthusiast for Hitler. He became Rector of the University of Freiburg, and gave a famous address on the centrality of the 'Fuhrer' to German renewal. Yet in 1947 Simone de Beauvoir still drew upon Heidegger's ideas to define the limits of tyranny, and there was a complex dialogue after the war with Sartre, to whose 'Existentialism and Humanism' Heidegger replied with his 'Letter on Humanism' (1946).

see also...

Anxiety; World

Heraclitus

In 1946, Martin Heidegger, barred from university teaching as a result of his support for Hitler while Rector of Freiburg University, wrote his famous 'Letter on Humanism'. At one point, he is engaged with the problem of the everyday world and the thinker. He re-tells a story from Aristotle about the early Greek philosopher, Heraclitus. Some enthusiasts came to visit the great thinker, and they found him warming himself by the open door of a bread oven. Surprised by this mundane figure, they questioned the sage, who replied that god, the divine presence, would show itself even here. Heidegger's biographer, Rüdiger Safranski, sees a strong identification between Heidegger and his ancient forebear. Certainly Heidegger goes on to credit Heraclitus with insights resembling his own, particularly with the argument that all of human existence is open to divine presence.

Heraclitus (c.521–487 BC) was one of a group known to historians as the 'pre-socratics', the philosophers before Socrates, and his disciple Plato. Heidegger repeatedly turns back to the pre-socratics, including Parmenides as well as Heraclitus, in whom he detected a care for being which deserted philosophy after them. In his *Introduction to Metaphysics* (originating 1935, published 1953), Heidegger picked out another saying from Heraclitus, in which 'war' becomes the universal 'father', the creator of everything in human life and nature. From this idea, Heidegger developed reflections on the disunity which is inseparable from existence. This ambiguous saying also preoccupied Nietzsche. Heidegger gave, and later published, courses on both Heraclitus and Parmenides.

Sartre also found himself in dialogue with the pre-socratics. In *Being and Time*, he picked out Heraclitus's most famous principle, that man cannot step into the same river twice, and subjects it to complex criticism. For Sartre, his ancient predecessor was even more sceptical than he himself, in denying all continuity to experience.

see also...

Becoming; Everyday

Hero

Existentialism often seems a negative philosophy. Accepted values are called into question or actively undermined. Experience is pulled out from inside the cocoon of meaning which we have wrapped around it. The predominant feeling is of coverings being pulled away to expose a reality that is often dark, always difficult. Yet Existentialism has not had a negative impact: on the contrary, its cultural associations are more dynamic than defeatist. One major reason that Existentialism has avoided being pigeon-holed as defeatist or pessimistic is the role it has played in expanding the idea of the hero.

The gallery of existential heroes ranges from Camus' Mersault, the outsider, who refuses to justify himself even in the face of execution, to Kierkegaard's Abraham, who risks total guilt for the Lord; from Sartre's Mathieu, who cannot find enough reasons for commitment, and yet will not settle for anything less, to de Beauvoir's Hélène, who is able to be both collaborator and resistance heroine; from Beckett's stoically irritable tramps to Dostoyevsky's self-annihilating underground man. None of these figures is a 'hero' in any traditional sense: they are not dashing or conventionally brave. Iris Murdoch uses the term 'the Existentialist hero', Camus talks of 'the absurd hero', and Kierkegaard calls it 'the knight of faith'.

At the heart of existential heroism is not so much an action as an attitude. Traditional heroes performed great deeds; existential heroes often fail to act, or are deprived of the chance to act, or find that their actions have been somehow taken out of their hands. It may seem a blessed release, as in the case of Kierkegaard's Abraham on the brink of child sacrifice, or it may seem torture, as in the case of Mersault, whose acts fall into the possession of others to interpret as they will. But as Murdoch says, the existential hero remains, in the face of both action and passivity, 'a person with no illusions and no certainties'. The one great achievement of these heroes is that they resist the temptation to settle for ordinary certainty.

see also...

Courage; Tragedy

Honesty

hy is 'to be honest' such a common phrase? The words slip into so many conversations: 'to be honest, I don't really like him ... I haven't a clue ... I couldn't care less'. Why do we keep saying it? Usually, when someone says 'to be honest', they are about to say something which might otherwise be unacceptable. The repeated catchphrase shows that at some level honesty is a more important virtue even than kindness, or competence, or concern, or duty. If you are being honest, then that cancels out the defect of being cruel or sloppy: well, that's what the words suggest. They invite the listener to smile or accept or tolerate what might be condemned.

Honesty has a similar status in existential thought. When in 1936 Karl Jaspers was trying to define the specific vision which had come into the world through Kierkegaard and Nietzsche, his existential ancestors, he declared that for such thinkers 'honesty is the decisive motivating factor'. In an existential life, the phrase 'to be honest' would have a new depth and meaning. Instead of being a hopeful excuse, it would become the one definite obligation

without which no other virtues are truly themselves. You can be brave without being honest, but then your bravery is just an aspect of your deceptiveness; you can be clever without being honest, and then your intelligence is just reduced to cunning. All other virtues are ambiguous for Jaspers, they depend on their situation; but from his existential viewpoint honesty is 'the minimum measure of the unconditional', the starting point for a life which can be accepted without qualification, on its own terms.

Yet honesty also seems an impossible requirement. In Sartre's *The Age of Reason*, Mathieu and Marcelle have resolved to be transparently honest together: but the result is endless uncertainty. Faced by her quizzical look at an important moment, he asks 'You think I'm lying to myself?' Her answer says it all, both honestly and evasively: 'No, anyway, one can't ever know.' Honesty turns out to be a question we have continually to ask ourselves, not a rule to be applied.

see also...

Bad Faith; Lies

Human Condition

'To avoid misunderstanding', declares the political theorist Hannah Arendt, 'the human condition is not the same as human nature'. Arendt, influenced by Heidegger and other Existentialists, was attempting to recreate the notion of 'the human condition' in order to find a new way to talk about what we have in common. The problem is that whenever we start talking about something which all human beings have in common, we tend to assume that this shared aspect is fixed and unchangeable. Terms like 'human nature' encourage this assumption that whatever people share together must always have been shared in the past, and always will be in the future. People have always been like that, we say, as we watch the latest images of a city destroyed, or see the young couple hand in hand down the street.

By 'human condition', Arendt means to start a discussion about the common field of human experience, without presupposing anything fixed or final. Even if you added up all 'human actions and capabilities' on view, you would never arrive at a complete list. Open the newspaper for one day. Look at the different ways of being human on offer: consumers are cautious, a general is impatient, a mother is relieved. Even in this land of types and shadows, there is no limit to the qualities and abilities on view. All are equally ways of being human, none more or less than the others. And in line with existential principle, Arendt goes on to argue that there are no 'essential characteristics of human existence in the sense that without them this existence would not be human'. You can take away reason, or you can subtract passion, you can rule out fear, or envy or any chosen favourite, and there will always be plenty of other human qualities to take their place.

The human condition is the shifting set of pressures and opportunities which invite us to act in some ways at some times, and prevent other actions in so doing. There is nothing fixed about this condition: it is the endlessly changing common ground of human action and thought.

see also...

Essence; Possibility

Humanity

It is hard not to think of our humanity as an accomplished fact of life. We are already human, before we start acting or thinking or choosing. But Existentialism resists this idea that the human precedes everything particular in our lives. Indeed for Existentialists our humanity lies ahead rather than behind. We are reaching out to grasp it, and in the process we are actively determining what it means to have humanity. One of the most extraordinary visions of this existential humanity comes from the religious thinker Berdyaev. He is presenting the future of Christianity, from the perspective of a believer. But for this believer, the faith itself is perpetually being remade, by the faithful. He looks towards a future in which Christianity will be reborn, and in that time 'the Spirit will have no holy scripture'. Faith will not root itself in a text. Nor will belief appear like a message from above. Instead, the Christian meaning 'will be accomplished in man and in humanity'.

The future of religion depends upon the power of man to recreate its meaning. In doing so, people will also recreate their own 'humanity'.

Berdyaev defines this future faith as 'an anthropological revelation': the meaning of this religion will be part of the meaning of humanity. If you want to understand this faith, you will have to inquire into the meaning of your own humanity, rather than into the messages of a sacred text. In a moment of supreme ambiguity, Berdyaev puts his hopes in an 'unveiling of the Christology of man.' In that new age, the meaning of Christianity would announce itself from inside the life of each person. The new sacred truths would be the same as the answers to the question: what is it that makes us human?

The psychiatrist and philosopher R D Laing gives a negative twist: if humanity can be created, it can also be denied to us. Laing redefines mental illness and other oppression as being 'bereft of humanity'. If our experience is denied, then we cannot make ourselves human in our own way.

see also...

Christian Existentialism; Creativity

I

What does it mean to be an individual, to be this particular person? Existentialism is important not so much because it has answered these questions, as because it has found rich ways of *asking* them. For example, Martin Buber approaches the question of individuality by asking: what does it mean when someone uses the word 'I', or its equivalent? After all, to be an individual person involves being able to speak for yourself in the first person: every language offers that possibility, in its own grammar.

Individuals are those in whose utterances the first person can find a home. But Buber then asks us to look again at that first person, that 'I'. He suggests that 'I' has two fundamentally different ways of being used: there are two distinct first persons. By this, he does not mean there are two grammatical rules or dictionary meanings. He means that people are doing one of two things when they take up their temporary home in the first person and say 'I' to the world, to others. They may be using either the word 'I-Thou' or the word 'I-It'. According to Buber, 'I-Thou' and 'I-It' are 'the primary words' in our lives. If your 'I' is an 'I-Thou', you are being yourself in the face of an equivalent person or presence. If your 'I' is an 'I-It', you are being yourself in a world which has no equivalent presence to your own, a world of objects not persons. So 'I-Thou' expects a reply, it is the 'I' of dialogue and responsiveness. You can give your view in a disagreement by saying 'I think you are wrong' in such a way as to recognize that the other will have his own response. You don't mean to imply doubt, but you do mean to allow the other to be present, to participate. Or you can say 'I think he is wrong', and make the other into a mere object of your commentary, an object which, if it speaks again, will merely be observed and judged like other objects, like a faulty machine not a wrong-headed person.

see also...

Address; Presence

Insecurity

You are at a party. Suddenly a stranger appears and, looking furious, insults you to your face, then leaves. There is an embarrassed silence. Then someone says, 'That's Bill, he's OK really, just insecure, so you never know what he'll do when he's had a few.' The excuse of insecurity, if it is an excuse, works easily when the person is aggressive or hostile, destructive or rude. 'Insecurity' is one of the greatest popular psychological catchphrases of our time. You can also apply it to yourself: if they only knew how insecure I really am!

The idea that 'insecurity' is a fundamental explanation for some kinds of behaviour has some of its deepest roots in Existentialism and particularly in the work of the existential psychologist R D Laing. Laing made a contrast between fundamental security and insecurity. This deep-level security and insecurity were to do with being itself: they were, in the terminology of Laing's argument 'ontological'. If you possessed primary security, then you had a settled relationship to the fact of your own being in the world; and, by contrast, if you were an example of primary insecurity, then you were denied any assured feeling of your own existence in the world. In a state of basic insecurity, you have no way of coming to terms with your own presence, or with the world which encloses you.

Laing did not intend these concepts as labels or as easy explanations, in the way that 'insecure' is used in ordinary conversation. This existential insecurity isn't just a flicker too much of anxiety, or a tendency to take offence. For those who are possessed by 'ontological insecurity', this condition is 'what being alive is like'. For these people, the world is continuously threatening. Therefore, they 'become absorbed in contriving ways of trying to be real'. Unpredictable aggression could betray such deep insecurity, but so could profound withdrawal. Moreover, there is something in each of us which can recognize this condition, which is perhaps the part of us that responds to Shakespeare's King Lear, Hamlet or Othello.

see also...

Anxiety; Therapy

Irony

We tend to think of irony as a style, a way of using words. Verbal irony consists of saying one thing but meaning another, or even the opposite. You talk of 'his typical generosity', and we all know what you mean. But within Existentialism irony has sometimes been seen as an approach to life, even a way of being a person. This approach to irony has had a deep influence on the modern idea of life as 'role playing'.

For Kierkegaard, in particular, and for later thinkers under his influence, notably the American philosopher Richard Rorty, the 'ironist' is able to live his life from within yet always aware that it is only one experience, only one perspective, and that other viewpoints will inevitably undermine all claims to absolute knowledge or insight or objectivity. Thus the ironist displays a kind of negative commitment, he is committed to realizing the limits of his own point of view, and of all other points of view insofar as they are themselves localized and limited. In Kierkegaard's character the Seducer, this irony has two levels. It is partly a deliberate attitude adopted to impress others:

'my irony at the foolishness of human beings …'. But there is a double irony, since the Seducer is aware that this attitude is itself a kind of pose, that there is something over-deliberate and arbitrary about it. Presenting himself as 'the ironist', the Seducer is always standing outside even that perspective. He will not even commit himself finally to his own irony. Irony means never being wholly at home inside any experience or perspective.

Richard Rorty uses the notion of irony to characterize the whole approach of key existential thinkers. For him, Kierkegaard, Nietzsche and Heidegger attempt to redescribe the world in a fresh way. Each has to take up an inherited language, and irony is their way of redefining the words and ideas as they use them. Yet why should the irony ever stop? Rorty believes the true ironist must cease to claim the last word. Here perhaps lies a future of Existentialism.

see also...

Commitment; Cynicism

Jaspers, Karl

Karl Jaspers (1883–1969) was one of the major figures in twentieth-century German philosophy. Before turning to philosophy he was originally trained in neuropathology and his work retains a strong psychological emphasis. Jaspers combines many major existential themes with a deeply religious sensibility. His important works include: *Philosophy* (1932), *Reason and Existenz* (1935), *Philosophy of Existence* (1938), *Of truth* (1946), The *Great Philosophers* (1957), *Philosophy is for Everyman* (1965).

Jaspers' work and life were movingly celebrated by his pupil Hannah Arendt. Jaspers was banned from his teaching post in 1938 by the Nazis, his wife Gertrud being Jewish and his ideas contrary to their requirements. The couple remained in Germany through the war, always on the verge of being consigned to concentration camps. For Arendt, as a Jewish philosopher, Jaspers stood through this time for 'inviolability'. Through his commitment to both love and thought, he kept open the rational space in what Arendt called 'dark times'. For the contemporary French thinker and writer Maurice

Blanchot, Jaspers' work presents to us 'a dialogue of existences', a vision in direct contrast to all totalitarian systems. Hans-Georg Gadamer, a leading modern German philosopher, associates Jaspers with the recognition that 'authority has nothing to do with obedience'. True authority derives from knowledge, freely recognized and open to question at all stages.

In *Philosophy*, Jaspers talks of risking everything in pursuit of total communication with the other. In this work, he urges upon us 'communication regarded as love'. Only in such communication, believes Jaspers, can any man hope to 'become himself'. Here the existential themes of freedom and becoming are woven together with a belief in communication. It is this communicative ethic which is perhaps the most influential legacy of Jaspers, together with his personal example.

see also...

Loss; Suicide

Justification

'How can a man be just before God?' asks Job in the Old Testament. The implication is that no one ever could be held 'just' in the face of a total and all-encompassing judgement. The question was given its existential, and also its modern, expression by Kierkegaard: 'How then does the individual assure himself that he is justified?' Kierkegaard was himself a religious thinker, and he was, in fact, writing about Abraham and Isaac; but it is all the more striking that he sees the lone person, facing the question of justification, without any clear context or court of appeal. For Job, the threat seems to be imminent condemnation; for Kierkegaard, the threat is rather an endless struggle with an impossible demand.

A company director is challenged to justify his 'huge pay rise' in the context of low wages. You are only ever called on to justify an action, or a life, if everything has been called in question. Justification is always the positive face put on a moment of extreme defensiveness. So Kierkegaard has posed the question, as often with Existentialism, in precisely the right way for our world: how could you ever get out of the situation into which you are plunged by the demand to justify yourself? In the face of this demand, one feels uncertain, one is permanently deprived of settled assurance.

Perhaps our jitteriness arises partly from the number of ways in which we are likely to face this terrible demand: justify yourself. Law courts may ask us, but so may professional bodies, or the media, or our customers, or our clients. But feeling all right about yourself is one of our ideals, and the demand for justification inevitably provokes the question: are we entitled to this feeling? The contemporary thinker, Jacques Derrida, argues that every decision is potentially unjustifiable, because there is a limitless range of alternatives. How could we ever show that any act was preferable to every single alternative? As we become more conscious of possibilities, so we find it ever harder to settle for any justification.

see also...

Reasons; Shame

Kierkegaard, Søren

Søren Kierkegaard (1813–55) was one of the most pervasive influences on later existential thinkers and writers, as well as on many other developments. He was born and lived in Denmark, and his work has exercised a global influence in translation among many languages. His major works include *Either/Or* (1843), *Fear and Trembling* (1843), *The Concept of Anxiety* (1844) and the *Concluding Unscientific Postscript to the Philosophical Fragments* (1846). Kierkegaard's influence is uniquely difficult to define. As Iris Murdoch notes, Sartre's work is everywhere coloured by Kierkegaard, yet he is nowhere acknowledged. In addition, others absorbed his influence into their lives, as well as their ideas. The German theologian Dietrich Bonhoeffer, who became involved in a plot to assassinate Hitler during the war, defined his acts in terms of Kierkegaard's concepts.

Karl Jaspers mapped the rise of existential thought in terms of the two key influences of Kierkegaard and Nietzsche. From Kierkegaard, declared Jaspers, came a new version of Christianity 'which is like a nothingness'. In his life, Kierkegaard was deeply in conflict with the established church, yet he shaped a modern conception of faith, in which absurdity, personal commitment and the leap of faith are central. These themes are explored in relation to the biblical story of Abraham and Isaac in *Fear and Trembling*. Here Kierkegaard presented an irreconcilable contradiction between faith and ethics, between authenticity and commonplace reasoning. In *Either/Or*, Kierkegaard mixes apparent autobiography, theory, fiction and polemic. Throughout there runs a problem of perspective, most vividly in the central section entitled 'The Seducer's Diary', where the narrator tells a tale of cruelty and seduction, which is also full of wisdom and mystery. At one point the Seducer ponders a man he seems to be manipulating and asks how all this appears 'in his own head'. This is a fundamental concern of Kierkegaard's thought: the inaccessible inwardness of each person's world.

see also...

Existential Leap; Faith

Knowledge

We have become accustomed to thinking that it is the destiny of the world to turn, eventually, into knowledge. For example, disease is always likely to yield to cure, given 'more research'. If a problem has not yet been solved, that is probably because we have not acquired the relevant expertise, but we could and, probably, will one day. We also think of this knowledge as acting upon the world, making change possible, creating options. A more knowledgeable person has more choices than a less informed one; to lack knowledge is to live a life deprived of potential. This assumption is most obvious in recent discussions of 'the information rich' and 'the information poor', as a result of access or lack of access to new technology.

Yet problems persist, in the face of our expanding knowledge. Nietzsche writes vividly of 'The shadow all things cast whenever the sunlight of knowledge falls upon them'. This metaphor suggests that you can only achieve extra illumination at the cost of accentuating the shadows. Knowledge is not, in this view, cost free, and it is wrong to think you could turn the whole world into a single system of knowledge. You can only understand one subject or event at the expense of clouding over another one nearby. For example, many of our cures have turned out to be problems in themselves. This does not mean we should abandon the cures, in Nietzsche's terms: there is no such thing as a world without shadows, there are no solutions which will not cause other problems somewhere else.

The light does brighten and, in some ways, the shadows deepen. Perhaps the most important example is the difference between our advances in technology and our understanding of people. It is precisely through the contrast with our expanding knowledge of technology that we feel how little we understand ourselves. But the result is that we can't tell the fate of all this technology. Finally, as Marcel puts it, for Existentialism, there is 'the primacy of being over knowledge': our world is older, and deeper, than our knowledge of it.

see also...
Being; Objects

Lack

Two teachers are discussing their classes. One says gloomily that his is such hard work, he cannot get anyone to concentrate for two minutes. The other replies that hers are a pleasure because they all 'want to learn'. They agree that this is what makes the difference: how can you teach children who don't want to learn?

What is involved in the idea of wanting to learn, which is one of the most important features of modern education? Seen in existential terms, before you can want to learn you must realize that something is missing from your life. There is something else which is still needed. You must see your life in terms of a lack before you want to learn: a lack of knowledge, or of understanding, or of capability. No one who sees their life as already complete will want to add anything to it. All that other knowledge, each new idea, will appear only as threatening presences.

It is strange to think positively of a lack. But in Existentialism, creativity is closely aligned with acknowledging a lack. De Beauvoir even argues that unless a person can make 'himself a lack of being' then he cannot throw his life forward into the world. She has a vivid image of a person who 'casts himself into the world', forwards in the search towards new experience, new knowledge, new ideas. Such a person wants to learn, whether in a classroom or beyond the educational setting. Usually, we think of a dynamic person as being self-confident, and stable. De Beauvoir asks us to consider the nature of self-confidence. Might there not, she is implying, be a confidence which is able to bear the possibility of being incomplete? This confidence would be able to leap into the space seen as a 'lack'. So back in that classroom, a child who sees her life as lacking a dimension of insight can throw herself forward in the hope of grasping new ideas. This leads de Beauvoir to an existential view of 'intelligence', which becomes 'a way of casting oneself into the world'.

see also...

Creativity; Existential Leap

Laing, R D

RD Laing (1927–89) was a psychiatrist, philosopher and writer, who achieved fame through his early book *The Divided Self* (1960), a radical reinterpretation of schizophrenia, mental distress and normality. This work drew directly and fully upon the existential thought of Sartre, Kierkegaard, Jaspers, Heidegger and others. Laing defined his aim as being to give an account 'in existential terms' of certain forms of madness. While preserving certain clinical and diagnostic terms, such as 'schizophrenia', Laing set out to achieve an inward understanding of individual experience. He hoped to grasp 'a person's experience of his world and of himself'. Pursuing this project, Laing developed concepts which expand the existential vision of individuality and emotion. He created a graphic picture of what he termed 'ontological insecurity', the lack of a substantial sense of self. This concept drew upon Heidegger's ideas on anxiety, and on Sartre's theory of 'the other'. But Laing gave the ideas a unique impact through his vivid sense of individual distress as presented to him in the course of his life as a psychiatrist and psychoanalyst. He also presented his positive response in terms of a concept of each individual's 'existential position'. Laing went on to write a wide range of influential books, reaching a large public audience on the topics of madness and sanity seen in increasingly social and even religious terms. In *The Self and Others* (1961) he focused on problems of communication, an approach closely related to the work of Karl Jaspers, with whom he had once planned to study. Other influential works include *The Politics of Experience and The Bird of Paradise* (1967) and *Knots* (1970). In *The Politics of Experience*, Laing used Existentialist concepts to explore creativity and its suppression in the modern world. For example, he invites us to wonder at the way individuality is forged, in a process 'enabling being to emerge from nothing'. In *Knots*, Laing presents a series of short poem-like fragments. For example, the comfort of 'One is inside' gets lost in a tide of anxiety, as 'One tries to get inside oneself'.

see also...

Existential Position; Insecurity

Lies

You are telling a lie when you say you have done something, and you actually have not got round to it. Or when you tell a person you like them when you don't. Lying, in this sense, is all about your words and how they affect another person. Existentialism has seized upon the idea of lying and developed it into a rich subject. The most powerful representative of 'the liar' in Existentialism is probably Dostoyevsky's 'underground man', the supposed author of *Notes From Underground*. He is obsessed by his own ability to tell lies. As a result, everything he says is haunted by the possibility of either being or even becoming a lie. Any statement is capable of being a lie, even if it is actually true. It is enough for the speaker to think it isn't true! … And any statement can feel like a lie if you change your mind in the middle. The effect is to make us realize that lying – and sincerity – are processes and not fixed states. Words, like lives, are in a process of becoming, and that includes becoming genuine or becoming fake.

So the underground man tells us he has been bad at his job, deliberately bad. Then he interrupts himself: 'I was lying when I just said that I was a bad civil servant.' And now we have to wonder: is he perhaps lying now? You suddenly realize how much trust is involved in any interpretation of what somebody else is telling you …

And then you realize something still more alarming about lies. You can never be quite sure that you are not telling them. For example, you say to a friend that you don't like someone you both know. It feels genuine, but afterwards you wonder whether you were trying to impress or to form an alliance … Then a whole life might become a fabric of such lies: 'I invented a life, so that I should at any rate *live*.' We are faced by the possibility that to be consciously alive is to inhabit a lie.

> ## see also...
> *Bad Faith; Negation*

Loss

Sadness is important to Existentialism. When you want something which you cannot have, then you might become frustrated or angry. You might feel unfairly treated or downright unlucky. But if you used to have this something, and you can't have it any longer, then you might become sad. Ordinary lives are full of both these kinds of absence: the things we cannot have, and the things we used to have and have lost. Some of these things, of course, are people, others are objects, and others are intangibles, like belief or status or the sense of belonging.

You might say that Marxism is the philosophy of the experience of being denied, the experience of never having. Existentialism is more the philosophy of the experiences of having lost, letting slip, of losing hold. Existentialists have been concerned to give voice to our experiences of disappearance and loss. For some existential thinkers those experiences are specifically definitive for modern life. So Paul Tillich insists that in the modern world 'man is still aware of what he has lost or is continuously losing'.

For Karl Jaspers, this sense of loss is present in some of the most terrible moments of the twentieth century. In his terms, we feel the loss of a centre, once called God, and so 'the value of man is also lost'. This in turn leads to endless losses, as if the world were literally being emptied: 'Any number of human beings are massacred because they are of no account.' It is as if humanity were being lost over and over again, in each atrocity.

For Tillich, our best resort is the art and thought which testifies to 'the profound experience of this loss', work of people like Auden and Sartre: it is these illuminations which may still lead to a new coming to terms with the unbearable losses of modern life. Within the experience of loss there still lies the potential for 'a liberation', a new creative responsibility for our own being. As Derrida puts it, the work of mourning is global at the end of the century.

see also...

Lack; Memory

Love

Two lovers are together. Each says: 'I love you' to the other. But how does either know what the other *means* by this word 'love'? Existentialism isn't content simply to accept this exchange of a word at face value. What is being shared here? How much can be shared? Simone de Beauvoir put the question in terms of a man and a woman: 'The word love has by no means the same meaning for both sexes.' But you could – as she also recognizes – extend the argument: why should this word ever mean the same thing for any two lovers? How much, we might add, do we need the other person to mean exactly what we mean? How far can we mean different things by it and still be in love together?

De Beauvoir explores some commonplace meanings of 'love'. She discerns a male tradition in which the word effectively means 'own', and 'I love you' is a statement of possession; and a female tradition in which it means a 'dream of annihilation'. But she states clearly, in existential terms, that there is nothing fixed or innate about such a division: it is due to the different social situations of the speakers. More interestingly, she goes on to offer a better sense of 'love', one which could be shared in an open-ended way. In her view, an 'authentic love' would 'accept the contingence of the other', his 'existence as an individual'. That is, for de Beauvoir, the meaning of 'love' would become redefined in terms of the other, the person addressed. It would be less about what is inside me, and more about a moment of complete recognition and acceptance of the other. The words 'I love you' would then be all about that 'you', and the meaning of the phrase would grow out of the specific encounter. 'Love' would be a different kind of word, facing outwards rather than inwards, connecting rather than separating. It would be a word in dialogue, a word which only made sense through a particular dialogue, 'the actual recognition of true liberty'.

see also...

Dialogue; Relationship

Marcel, Gabriel

abriel Marcel (1889–1973) was the major French voice of 'Christian Existentialism', a term which he adopted with some reluctance. His influence was at its height in the immediate post-war period, when he seemed to offer an alternative to the radical atheism of Sartre for those believers or agnostics who wished to adopt an existential approach. Marcel's major works include: *The Philosophy of Existence* (1948), *The Mystery of Being* (1951), *Man Against Society* (1952).

When, in 1950, Iris Murdoch was trying to persuade English and American philosophers that there might be legitimate alternatives to their approach, she turned to the example of Gabriel Marcel. At that time, Anglo-American philosophy emphasized logic and the detailed analysis of propositions. For many in that tradition, 'continental' philosophy seemed dangerously emotive and metaphorical. Murdoch, while sharing many Anglo-American ideals, argues that a thinker like Marcel is also 'a modern moral philosopher' who himself has 'new and persuasive concepts'. She defends his right to employ such terms as 'mystery' and

'participation' in the course of philosophical argument. She even finds in Marcel a 'genius' for describing in philosophical terms the recognizable quality of our human experience. Marcel becomes the example of philosophy that is concerned with the individual life, rather than with abstract and universal formulae.

Marcel was certainly a lively and courageous arguer. He stood his ground in the face of the huge status of Sartre and defended his religious view of being with vigour. In *The Philosophy of Existence*, Marcel began from 'the primacy of being over knowledge': no certainties are given in advance. Yet he also insisted that 'I am not my life', that there remains something left over when all the circumstances and experiences have been catalogued. From here he makes his existential defence of faith. In *Man Against Society*, he demanded a concern for freedom in the present, as against fruitless definitions of an 'essential notion' of freedom.

see also...

Christian Existentialism; Presence

Meaning

According to the theologian Paul Tillich, Existentialism arises from 'the experience of meaninglessness'. You did not have to be a specialist in philosophy, or a writer of anguished fiction to share the experience of meaninglessness: all you had to do was live in the modern world. In this widely influential definition, Existentialism is about something lacking from our lives, and 'meaning' is one of the most important names for this lack. If we all endure this deprivation, then, whether we are fully aware or not, we are all Existentialists now. The role of the existential philosophy, or approach, is to give full expression to this predicament, perhaps in the hope of overcoming the meaninglessness, if not, in the determination to face it directly.

There is, of course, something potentially ridiculous in going on and on about how life has no meaning. Leading Existentialists were aware of the risks of pomposity and complacent gloominess. Iris Murdoch saw clearly how Existentialism might appear, if the discussion of meaning and its loss became too familiar: 'One must ask … why all this fuss, all this talk about 'meaning'?' Indeed a flaw in Existentialism has been its tendency to encourage too fluent a discussion of 'meaning' and 'meaninglessness', in which the terms themselves become clichés. The danger in this talk of meaning and its absence is that ordinary frustrations and worries become magnified in a glamorous psychobabble, of the kind exploited and parodied by Woody Allen, where a bungled dinner date turns into the defeat of Western civilization.

But Existentialists were capable of being both precise and lively about the problems of meaning. The trouble is, says Murdoch, that we now have to start the search for meaning within our personal consciousness. But, unlike the solid looking churches and authorities of the past, this consciousness is shadowy and even flimsy. I turn to my thoughts and ask them to come up with a meaning, but 'consciousness … is not a substance and it has no meaning'. Each of us has to create meaning, starting with nothing: we are all conjurers now.

see also...

Loss; Superman

Memory

Imagine living without a memory for anything which you have done or seen or said. Mysteriously, you still remember everything general: your command of language is perfect, your general knowledge flawless. But at a personal level, each moment is a fresh start, isn't it? Nothing carries the burden of association, you are not limited by all the commitments you have previously made, to others and to yourself. Would this not be perfect existential freedom, are you not free to become whatever you choose in every moment of your life?

The lure of this personalized amnesia has been felt by Existentialists. Kierkegaard asked himself, and us, whether it would not be an ideal life in which you could forget yourself and endlessly 'become something new'. Milan Kundera took the question forward to a political level, by considering a State which can erase its tracks as it moves forward, or seems to. But the political consequence of living without personal memory was, he felt, totalitarianism not freedom; and the personal consequence seemed, for his predecessor Kierkegaard, no less disastrous. Why does this amnesia not mean pure freedom?

According to Kierkegaard, to be bereft of personal memory would reduce you to the level of an animal, even if you are an animal with up-to-date general information and articulacy. The argument about amnesiac liberation takes us to the heart of Existentialism and its concept of painful freedom. In this approach, freedom means nothing in the abstract. It is only as myself that I can be free. But if I have no memory of my own acts and thoughts, then I have no self. For a being without such a self, freedom is a foreign language.

Above all, without personal recall you could not experience faith, nor even decision. To have faith means to sustain a vision in the face of change and challenge; to decide means to live through the outcomes of your decision, and to know that you will do so when you are deciding. Memory burdens us with an individual condition, but it also makes our freedom possible.

see also...

Freedom; Time

Moods

We tend to talk as if having 'moods' were an obstacle to attaining real understanding or living a balanced life. Why is he refusing to fit in? Oh, never mind, it's just one of his moods, you know. In other words, a mood is a temporary aberration, a passing disturbance in the even substance of a person. While a person is possessed by a mood, they had better not be treated as if they were a reasonable being. This isn't only true of bad moods. Cheerfulness too can be a mood, if it seems to have no basis in anything reasonable: it's just a passing determination to look on the brighter side, which might make someone dangerously over-optimistic.

It seems to follow that only in the intervals between these mysterious moods are we in touch either with ourselves or with reality. Existentialists are bound to be suspicious of this model of human experience: it is too flat, and too dismissive of the range of our possibilities. Heidegger is particularly firm in his defence of moods: 'Understanding has its moods,' he says. In other words, you don't achieve understanding by waiting for a moment which seems to be uncoloured by any mood. Understanding, for Heidegger, derives from moods. Understanding is one way in which a mood can express itself. There is no alternative to this moodiness in understanding.

You are having a conversation with a stranger, say about a general topic, like the environment. You can tell some things about this person, from a smart suit, or untidy hair. But the conversation has not come into focus yet. Then he lets slip that he owns a plastics factory, or lives on a rural commune. You feel at that point: 'Oh now I understand,' you know why he is saying these things and where they will lead. This is a moment of understanding, but it is always coloured by a surrounding atmosphere. You might feel annoyed, or relieved; you might feel dismissive or supported. But there is no experience of understanding which comes before those colouring influences, these moods.

see also...

Emotion; Knowledge

71

Murdoch, Iris

Iris Murdoch (1919–99) was one of the leading English post-war novelists, as well as a major philosopher. Her involvement with Existentialism is most explicit in her book *Sartre: The Romantic Rationalist* (1953) and in many essays collected in the volume *Existentialists and Mystics* (1999). Her many novels are also closely involved with existential ideas, a key example being *The Black Prince* (1973), a subtle narrative written from the point of view of a man condemned, wrongly, for a murder. In this work Murdoch engages in a sustained dialogue with Camus' *The Outsider*. As the contemporary American philosopher Martha Nussbaum observes, Murdoch's outlook weds together philosophy and fiction into a single process, an achievement which bears comparison with the work of Sartre. The literary critic George Steiner reports that Iris Murdoch was engaged on a study of the existential philosopher Martin Heidegger before her final illness. Murdoch's work serves, among many other things, to connect English philosophy and fiction with the continental currents that include Existentialism.

In her study of Sartre, Murdoch explored the interplay between Existentialism and Marxism in post-war Europe. She examined Sartre's transition towards Marxism, showing both the connections and the contrasts with his thorough-going existential phase previously. The book is particularly notable for the interweaving of Sartre's fiction and philosophy, and it is perhaps this interconnection which was of most lasting importance to Murdoch. For example, Murdoch draws together both Sartre's theories and his stories into a vision of individual isolation, where each person 'touches others at the fingertips'. This is a vivid and moving example of Murdoch's sensitivity to the metaphors of existential thought. Elsewhere, in an essay of 1952, she talks of 'the Existentialist mythology', meaning not something illusory but a world vision akin to a religion or a culture.

see also...

Hero; Meaning

Negation

Negation is a type of action, often performed using language. To negate means to deny, to contradict, to criticize. As human beings, we possess the power of negation, of overturning, or reversing, aspects of the world. This power to negate is tied up with certain aspects of language, most obviously with negative words like 'not' and 'no'. Of course you can contradict or deny without using any direct negatives: 'I believe he is honest' could be a negation if the previous speaker has said 'He's a real liar.' Nevertheless, we get our basic understanding of negation starting from the directly negative expressions.

Existentialism has been deeply preoccupied with the power of negation, partly because it is hard to imagine that any other species possesses it in the way we do. Since Existentialists are committed to exploring the human without prior definitions or limits, such a potential common feature is intriguing. What does it tell us about human being, if it is distinguished by this power of negation, this capacity to engage with the world through what is not believed, not seen, not accepted?

Heidegger suggests there is no human intellect without negation. But then he argues that negation itself must have origins somewhere else. The fact that language involves negation must tell us something deeper about the world in which this language has arisen. For Heidegger, 'the nothing is the origin of negation'. Here he is referring to the idea that in the world there is a basic opposition between 'being' and 'nothing'. You can form an idea of existence only in relation to non-existence; you can grasp some things only by seeing the absence of other things. And this is true of the world as a whole: you can form an idea of this world, only by contrast with its total absence, with nothing. It is this 'nothing' which has seeped into language in all the negatives and ways of negating, but without them, we could not reason. Our reasoning has origins in the void, the epitome of all that is beyond rational comprehension.

see also...

Nothing; Reasons

73

Nietzsche, Friedrich

Nietzsche (1844–1900) is most famed for the announcement by his character Zarathustra, in *Thus Spake Zarathustra*, that 'God is dead'. His father was a Protestant pastor, and this seems to speak of a deep alienation. But in many ways, Nietzsche was a profoundly traditional thinker: his work is suffused with classical and biblical echoes, and he uses many literary forms from earlier times, including philosophical dialogues and parables, epigrammatic paradoxes and symbols. His key works include: *The Birth of Tragedy From the Spirit of Music* (1872), *Untimely Meditations* (1873), *The Will to Power* (1895), *Human, All Too Human* (1876/86), and *Thus Spake Zarathustra* (1883/91). These display an astonishing range of both form and content, which has led Jacques Derrida to celebrate Nietzsche as the true discoverer of the 'heterogeneity' of writing itself: it is as if the endless play of different voices and styles that characterizes a whole civilization has been re-created within one author's work.

The same baffling diversity is evident in the reception of Nietzsche's work.

The Nazis placed a high value upon *Zarathustra* in particular. Yet Nietzsche's reputation has survived this association, and he is held in high esteem, for instance, by the contemporary liberal philosopher Richard Rorty and by the anti-totalitarian novelist Milan Kundera. Rorty stakes a strange claim for Nietzsche, arguing that he was the first major thinker who taught us to cease searching to know 'the truth'. Instead we should pursue the way of self-creation. For Karl Jaspers, Nietzsche's vision was that 'it is up to us to see what we become through ourselves'. This emphasis upon individual responsibility passes from Nietzsche into later existential thought. Other thinkers, though not seeing Nietzsche as a proto-fascist, nonetheless remain suspicious that, as the contemporary German thinker Habermas argues, he has abandoned reason in pursuit of mythology.

In Nietzsche, insight is inseparable from ambiguity: Zarathustra says that we hear the fountains only at night.

---

see also...

Knowledge; Superman

Nothing

Think of all the commonplace phrases that involve the word 'nothing'. If you reluctantly accept something, it is 'better than nothing'; if you help, 'it's nothing'; if you don't care, 'it's nothing to me'; if there is no choice, then 'there is nothing for it'; if this is the decisive moment, 'it's all or nothing'; if you find it easy, 'there's nothing to it'. The catalogue rolls on: 'nothing less (than), 'nothing other (than); 'nothing I would rather (do)'. It seems that we are continually relating our lives to 'nothing'. The word 'nothing' slips endlessly into our everyday lives.

In Beckett's play *Endgame*, two characters exist in an empty room, with only parent-filled dustbins for company. One exclaims that a certain way to pass the time would be 'better than nothing'. The other replies with amazed disbelief: how could anything be better than nothing? Suddenly, you notice the words, and especially the 'nothing' which has been there all the time. This effect is representative of Existentialism more generally, in the way it draws attention to the nothing which we like to pass over. Beckett will not allow us to avert our ears from the many nothings with which we fill our everyday language.

Like Beckett's characters, we exist in relation to nothing. Beckett is defining for us, probably to our dismay, what Heidegger calls 'nothing pure and simple'. This is the nothing which lies opposite everything. But nothing is not simply outside, it is everywhere a part of our living. Sartre refers to the many different kinds of nothing which help to fill our lives. One vivid example is 'that nothing which insinuates itself between motives and act'. We have motives: say,
I want to impress the neighbours, and that's why I buy this new car. But there is always a gap between the general motive and the specific act: I could have done an infinite number of other things for the same reasons, and I could have bought this shiny blue vehicle for an infinite number of other motives. The name for this particular nothing is human freedom.

see also...

Anguish; Negation

Objects

Objects have a strange status in Existentialism. Whatever its variety, Existentialism is committed to not overlooking the realm of objects, in favour of some other or supposedly higher region. But, on the other hand, Existentialists often use the idea of 'the object' negatively, especially where people are concerned. So when Heidegger wants to provoke us to start thinking about 'the world', he declares 'the first step is to enumerate the things that are 'in' the world: houses, trees, people, mountains, stars'. The list incites further reflection: people both are and are not *in* the world in the same way as stars or trees. How do we figure in relation to the world of objects?

Consider a memory. I remember a room, with a person sitting in a chair. I can recall all the externals, the material of the curtains, the cracks in the window glass. The person is also vividly present to me. But there is something different about the way memory casts this person back into my life, as compared to the way the other objects return. The religious Existentialist, Gabriel Marcel, put the contrast in terms of a distinction between object and presence: 'presence … is *more* than the object, it exceeds the object on every side.' This person was present for me in a different way from even the most important of familiar objects. So now, in the memory, I still have a different experience of this person and the room which encloses him. He is there with the other objects, a body in the chair, beneath the window. But he returns also as a whole being, and as such he engages my whole being in experience. He both is and is not there in the same way as the setting: his presence flows around his image. I cannot recall, according to Marcel's way of thinking, this person without a feeling of present-ness, what his presence would be like; whereas the objects evoke only detailed associations.

Jaspers warned that though human sciences must illuminate man 'as an object', yet our human awareness always eludes that external knowledge.

see also...

Equipment; Reality

Others

'The Other' is one of the strangest terms used by Existentialists, and one they have most in common. What does the term mean? 'Other' is really a position occupied by many different people and beings in the life of any individual. The Other is not any one of these figures, it is all and none of them. The Other is that towards which we orient our being, with hope or love, with fear or boredom. Individuals and perhaps whole cultures have ways of relating to the Other which surpass any particular occasion or relationship.

Take the archetypal situation, the one which seems to haunt the existential imagination. There are two people present, and they are in contact, across a space that both separates and connects them. I am here on this side, and my whole being is engaged in this unspoken dialogue. One finds this scene in de Beauvoir, Camus, Heidegger, Nietzsche, Kierkegaard, Dostoyevsky, Auden, Beckett: but the most intense realization occurs in the work of Sartre. The whole complex philosophy of his massive *Being and Nothingness* seems to turn upon the scene where I and Other

interconnect: 'the Other is not only the one whom I see but the one who sees me'. All kinds of details cover over this fundamental drama, in modern society. We are busy being at work, or being consumers, or developing a relationship: but in the midst of all the complexity there is this central moment of the double look, I to Other, Other to me. In that exchange, both beings are being re-defined. If I am in command of my life, then I can enter into thousands of such exchanges in every day of my life, indeed I must do so. These are the countless moments in which I experience myself as a person in the world, involved with Others and so able to be myself. But if I lack this command, if it falters or is lost, then the 'other' can 'appear to us as organizing our experience'. In that moment 'I' am lost to myself.

see also...

Dialogue; Shame

Possibility

Two people meet. There is a flicker of interest, though neither knows anything much about the other. What is such interest about? How can you feel interested before you know anything? The same question applies to other experiences of interest: why does one sometimes feel gripped by a book after the first sentence, even though one knows nothing about what it means or what is coming next? Why do some ideas compel one's attention, when so many others drift past in a haze of indifference? Existentialism approaches this question of interest and involvement by way of the idea of 'possibility'.

For Kierkegaard, the moment on the threshold of an involvement, say in a relationship, is one of 'infinite possibility'. That is how he defines, through one of his narrators, called the Seducer, the very meaning of 'the interesting'. To be interested is to experience a sudden expanding of the world, an expansion caused not by anything definite, but by questions and hints, signs and suggestions. Possibility is what draws us forwards, ahead of our knowledge or understanding: towards the person, into the book, after the idea.

But what happens next? As we enter into the next phase, when the relationship develops, or the book is being read, we either pull back or we 'are thrust' into the situation, in Sartre's terms, and find ourselves 'engaged'. In this engagement we constantly discover new possibilities: they are found within the experience itself, they have no presence outside it. These possibilities are not vague plans or speculations. They are what keeps us there, deepening the intimacy, enriching the reading, expanding the idea. These possibilities are, ultimately, ways of enriching our own being: they are aspects of our own life which we can only encounter through this relationship, this book, this thought. To add the voice of R D Laing, a rich engagement actually expands our whole existence. In the fruitful intimacy, new possibilities are disclosed; in the creative action, we discover ourselves to be larger than we thought before. Conversely, in the barren encounter, the false pathway, we become shrunken.

> ## see also...
> *Action; Becoming*

Presence

You are surrounded all the time by the effects of your own presence on the world. Imagine your life transformed into a video: you are invisible, but virtually everything that appears is in some way or other affected by you. Faces smile or frown, people approach or leave, objects come and go. De Beauvoir's hero Blomart describes a life in these terms: ' 'Everywhere I beheld the uneasy signs of my presence.' Presence is the presentation of your being to this outside world. It is towards your presence that these expressions were cast, these actions directed. Presence is the outward expression of our lives, the possibility of our being experienced as parts of other people's world.

Therefore, as de Beauvoir's speaker realizes, our presence is one thing that we cannot experience directly. You can only tell about it from the reactions of others, the effects in the world. When the day began, this was a tidy room; now it is a jumble, busy and also messy. That is one of the signs by which I recognize something about my own presence in the world. The experience is also uneasy because at times the 'signs' don't fit with our own sense of ourselves. People look nervous, when we think we are reassuring. They look bored when we think we are fascinating. Then presence seems almost like a trap, and de Beauvoir has her character feel desperation in the face of this idea, that 'he would never extend beyond the opacity of his own presence'. The world is forever tainted by this presence, he will never have any experience of a world which is not already affected by this presence. He longs to experience a world free of his own effects: but everything around him tells the tale of his own passage through that world.

Could a thinker escape the trap of his own presence through ideas, especially through writing? The writer and philosopher Maurice Blanchot evokes the ideal of 'suspending, or making disappear, every present and all presence'. But such thinking or writing suppresses its own origins, a necessary presence.

see also...
Nothing; Objects

Purpose

Dostoyevsky's 'underground man' is probably the strangest of all existential characters. He sits alone and tells us of his strange world. For this character, purpose is the weirdest thing about other people. He sees them all engaged in striving after their goals, reaching towards their ideals, snatching at their aims. He sarcastically remarks that 'man is an animal predominantly constructive'. It is the way these people seem to be: they devote their lives to building a road, to putting up a bridge, to making the next construction stand up. It is these purposes that enable people to live reasonable-seeming lives. What they do makes sense in the light of their aims and goals. But, wonders this strange, dissociated speaker, where does the sense of purpose come from in the first place? It seems to him that these people are possessed by the idea of purpose long before they form any particular aim or project. Therefore, however reasonable their plans or targets, there is at bottom something eerie and irrational in their whole purposeful engagement. The one thing which they have not taken into consideration is the value of purpose in general: they just leap straight in to pursue this or that goal.

As a result, reflects the underground man, they are often dissatisfied when they succeed. It is the purpose that gives meaning to their lives: success takes away that meaning, and then their lives are empty. A student dedicates himself to succeeding in an exam: when he does so, that purpose is used up. Unless another one takes its place, then the result is a lethargic collapse. Or take the head teacher who has devoted herself to making the school shape up. The inspection is passed with flying colours: and then what? For the underground man, the whole of a society can be in such a state. He describes St Petersburg as 'the most abstract and intentional city' on earth. As the guiding purposes are fulfilled, the city becomes less and less alive. Is this not an aspect of modern progress itself, this empty fulfilment of long-held purposes?

see also...

Commitment; Irony

Questions

In Samuel Beckett's play *Waiting for Godot*, Vladimir and Estragon, two tramp-like figures, are stranded on stage for the duration, with occasional interventions from other characters. They are, as the title says, waiting for a mysterious visitation, a possible rescue or redemption. Despite the arrival of Godot's messenger boy, he himself never appears. In the midst of this suspended interval, Vladimir asks himself 'what are we doing here?', and he reflects '*that* is the question', in an echo of Hamlet's famous 'to be or not to be/That is the question'. Vladimir adds quickly, and unlike Hamlet, that they are 'blessed', since they happen to have the answer. They are waiting for Godot. In other words, they are there because that's where they are staying.

The word 'answer' arouses immediate suspicion in an existential context. Existentialists have been distrustful of answers. It is not the question which traps Vladimir, it is his belief that he has been blessed with the answer. The question might allow him to move, even to move on. The answer keeps him in place. In some ways, this is the reverse of normal thinking, in which questions make us dither and delay, and answers are decisive and dynamic. In the existential world, as re-created by Beckett, answers are static: they are endings, limits, and as such they are false to experience.

We tend to link action with answers, and inaction with questions. But it might be that questioning is the most truly active way to be, and that answers allow us to disguise our inertia in habitual actions. At a more general level, we tend to assume that truth is an answer, but might it not be a question instead? Could the truth not take the form of just the right question asked in exactly the true way? Karl Jaspers sees the true thinkers as searching for 'that which puts everything into question'. Real insight here means not having all the answers, but understanding how everything can be questioned. Through this principle, the Existentialism of Jaspers and others has profoundly influenced modern education.

see also...

Hero; Lack

Reality

'The reality of that cup is that it is there and that it is not me.'

Sartre

This is one of the most intriguing statements in Existentialism. Usually, the question of 'reality' is presented as if it were extremely abstract or complex. 'What is reality?' sounds like exactly the kind of problem which makes philosophy remote from everyday experience. But for Sartre, reality is not an abstract concept. It is a certain way of experiencing things, it is almost a sensation. Reality is an impact which things have on you when you come into contact with them.

So reality belongs to specific objects in the world. You can talk about the reality of that cup, rather than reality in the abstract. Reality is not something that is added to the cup from outside, or that is found lurking somewhere behind things. Reality is what it seems to be. Many philosophies would see reality as distinct from our perception of individual objects like cups and so on. Reality might be permanent, even eternal, where these things are temporary and changing. So the

reality of the universe would be that which does not change; and the world of cups and things would be either unreal or at best a semblance of reality. In the modern scientific age, one could think of the real cup as atoms buzzing or as patterns of energy or as chemical formulae. But for Sartre, these added facts would not undermine the status of the thing we see, there: that is the reality of the cup. And the way you can tell is that you experience it as 'not me', as independent of your will. It confronts you in the negative: somewhere between here and there the 'me' has ended and other realities have come into play, like that of the cup.

But the cup is only 'not me' when I am looking at it. If someone else is looking, it becomes not them. It is real but its reality is relative to the observer. This cup is real for me in my way and for you in yours.

see also...

Appearances; Negation

Reasons

Existentialism is not an anti-rational philosophy, and few Existentialists have consistently advocated being unreasonable as a solution to life's problems. On the other hand, Existentialism repeatedly does draw attention to the limits of reason, and to the power of non-rational influences in human life. In everyday life, reason shows itself most clearly in our power to give, and to find, specific reasons for what we are doing, for how we are and are not acting or living. People are very adept at providing reasoned explanations to others, and to themselves. Indeed, we are good at coming up with alternative reasons, if some seem shaky. We live our lives in a cloud of useful reasons. They cover small decisions: I'll take the car today, it looks like rain. And they cover big decisions: I'll emigrate next year, because I must have more sunlight and space. We are rarely short of a reason, for long.

Here lies the problem with reason and reasons, from an existential point of view. Karl Jaspers warns that our reasons have 'the tendency to seduce us into a state of satisfaction': reasons are ways of living with what

we choose. By contrast, Jaspers points towards a certain 'dissatisfaction' which has no basis in 'generally valid reasons'. Jaspers takes the side of the nebulous dissatisfaction against the host of valid reasons. He believes we need to take our dissatisfaction more seriously, and our reasons less seriously.

A different problem with reason emerges when Sartre's hero Mathieu Delarue is confronted by the committed Communist Brunet, who appeals to him to join the Party. In the Europe of the late 1930s, fascism is on the march. The appeal seems tempting. Mathieu, in many ways a lost soul, but a tough intellect, replies that he hasn't 'enough reasons' to join, though his feelings are strong. Sartre seems to imply that to someone who is honest there never are enough reasons. You could call this an impasse. Or you could say that we need to pass beyond the reasons. Where the reasons stop, we have to assume purely personal responsibility.

see also...

Anguish; Choice

Relationship

'Relationship' is one of the most important words in contemporary culture. Relationships are central to our ideas about a good life. The good life, for our contemporaries, is one rich in relationships. But there are different views of what makes a good or desirable relationship: stability, excitement, surprise, security. In other words, our debate about what makes for the good life is primarily conducted in terms of what makes for a good relationship. Existentialism both anticipates and enriches this language of relationships. As Martin Buber put it, at the most general: 'In the beginning is relation'. We start the world oriented towards relationships: in many ways, relationship is our word for world.

Kierkegaard was a great existential explorer of this modern ideal, the relationship. In his strange *Seducer's Diary* many modern developments are anticipated. The narrator approaches a young girl with hope: 'so much the more I promise myself from this relationship'. A relationship is a promise, a goal, a way of giving meaning to life. There is also a deep contradiction in the modern word relationship. It involves another person, yet it is often seen as part of my personal satisfaction. In that case, the other could simply become a means to my goals. This is the down side of the relationship culture. As a famous self-help guide puts it: get what you want from your relationships. So Kierkegaard creates a character who is obsessed with relationships, yet all the more isolated in his own pursuits. Part of the modern idea of a relationship is that it is not based on external frameworks: it is a choice, a realm of free commitment. So the seducer breaks off a formal engagement 'so as to ensure a more beautiful and more significant relationship'. This is the seduction, a moment of pure exploitation. The freedom is one-sided, in this world of self-seeking relationships. The implied contrast is with true reciprocity where relationship is mutually constructed. Buber longs for a world where every greeting will involve this kind of authentic relation: he celebrates the African 'I see you!'

see also...

Community; Love

Responsibility

esponsibility can come with the job. You have been appointed, say, to take responsibility for ticket sales. Such responsibility is defined from outside: the definition covers what you will do, what will happen if you don't do it, and also who you are responsible *to* within the organization. One can call this an external notion of responsibility, and it is the reverse of an existential idea of being responsible.

In existential terms, one has to begin by taking responsibility for the definition itself: no one else can determine for you where your responsibility in life begins and whether it ends. For an inheritor of Existentialism, like Jacques Derrida, external responsibility actually makes people irresponsible, by lifting from them the primary burden, the big question: do you hold *yourself* responsible? For Derrida, a society where everyone knows the nature and the limits of their responsibilities in advance is breeding respectable-looking mayhem. No one will feel accountable to himself for anything, finally, in such a world. For Derrida, there is no authentic escape from 'the responsibility that consists in

always being alone'. With the triumph of external responsibility, it will be enough to be able to give a standard explanation of why you acted as you did, in the required terms. In the world of organized responsibility, all 'singularity' is dissolved; only systems and functions are called in question. The inner dialogue of responsibility is silent; instead, there is a stately and formal dance of acceptable explanations.

De Beauvoir makes one of her characters, a resistance leader, react to the Nazi invasion by feeling this: 'Women and new-born children die in the ditches … Because of me. Each of us is responsible for everything.' This last sentence is quoted from Dostoyevsky: it epitomizes the inner, existential vision of total responsibility. The news comes onto our screens, and we see far-off catastrophes, for which we cannot be held to account. However, we can still hold ourselves accountable, there is a perspective from which we might have lived differently.

see also...

Consequences; Freedom

Revolution

When Nietzsche demanded that we devote ourselves to 'overcoming' life as we are given it, he made a revolutionary appeal. In this sense, Existentialism has always been profoundly revolutionary. However the prevailing conditions are defined, Existentialists have asked us to go beyond, to transform, to leap over into a changed world. Conversely, Existentialism has tended to portray negatively those who settle for, or endorse as inevitable, the existing arrangements. This is as true of the Catholic Marcel as of the politically radical de Beauvoir or Fanon. Of course, such thinkers mean different things by their demand for transformation. Marcel looks to a new spiritual authenticity; Nietzsche to the coming of the Superman; de Beauvoir to the overcoming of social oppression; and Fanon to the ending of colonized worlds.

In Existentialism, revolution is seen in terms that reach beyond politics, including the most influential revolutionary politics of the Left. De Beauvoir developed an existential theory of revolution, in which the idea extends beyond Marxist political ideals, though in dialogue with them. For de Beauvoir, it is necessary to distrust the 'serious revolutionary', because he refers everything entirely to the one idea, of the total revolution. But no idea can resolve all questions. The political ideologue forgets that 'the revolutionary enterprise has a human meaning'. De Beauvoir finds it plausible that only a revolution could sweep away the all-encompassing oppression of the modern world. But she believes the meaning of any such revolution is created by those involved; and she distrusts those who wish the ideal of revolution to give meaning to their lives, as if from the outside.

De Beauvoir also applies an existential approach to the ethics of revolution. She warns the serious revolutionary that 'none of his particular decisions involves the revolution in its totality'. The revolution is itself a choice, and not a given fact of history. As the poet Auden put it, 'History' cannot 'help or pardon' us; neither our successes nor our failures can be redeemed.

see also...

Ambiguity; Superman

Sacrifice

When I asked a group of my students to write down their most highly rated action, the most popular answer turned out to be 'self-sacrifice', whose extreme form was dying on behalf of others or another person. But then you wonder: are all self-sacrifices equally good? Does it matter what you have sacrificed yourself on behalf of? Or is the act itself inherently valuable? The more you think about it – the more we did think about it – the more ambiguous self-sacrifice becomes. If it retains its appeal then perhaps that is because self-sacrifice is so diametrically the opposite of the common-sense logic by which we have learnt to live our lives, the logic of self-interest within civilized limits.

Existentialism has been repeatedly preoccupied with both sacrifice and self-sacrifice, and one of the main reasons is this contrast with conventional values and assumptions. Kierkegaard was entranced not by Abraham's willingness to sacrifice his son Isaac to God, but by his self-sacrifice in the process. Nietzsche asked more brutal questions, and got tougher answers. He argues that people will always prefer to make 'a great sacrifice' rather than a little one, if they have the choice, not because they are truly selfless but because they can reap the reward of self-congratulation. Small sacrifices remain irritating, because you can't take much pride in them. Large ones give us a real glow of self-liking, and so they turn out to be easier psychologically. Giving away your umbrella in the rain may rankle long after giving that cheque to the charity appeal has become a misty glow.

In recent existential thinking, the idea of sacrifice has taken another turn. In the view of Jacques Derrida, I am able to bear the thought of my life only because I ignore 'the infinite sacrifice I make at each moment'. My life is like a long walk down a street lined by beggars whom I disregard. These beggars include all the better choices, as well as all the unnoticed demands. In this perspective, self-sacrifice is always outgunned in advance.

see also...

Justification; Responsibility

Sartre, Jean-Paul

Jean-Paul Sartre (1905–80) was a leading figure in twentieth-century philosophy, literature and politics. His ideas evolved ceaselessly, and Existentialism played a crucial role in that evolution. The major works of Sartre's most explicitly and commitedly existential phase include: the metaphysical novel *Nausea* (1938), the philosophical system *Being and Nothingness* (1943), the *Roads to Freedom* trilogy [*The Age of Reason* (1945), *The Reprieve* (1945) and *Iron in The Soul* (1949)] and the influential summary *Existentialism and Humanism* (1946). His subsequent key works include *Critique of Dialectical Reason* (1960) and biographical philosophies of Genet, Baudelaire and Flaubert.

Called up, Sartre was captured without action in 1940 and held in a prisoner of war camp. On his release, he returned to Paris, and in this period, living in the same hotel as Simone de Beauvoir with whom he shared a sustained dialogue, he worked out a personal and philosophical vision. This outlook had already found preliminary expression, notably in *Nausea*, which Iris Murdoch called 'a sort of hate poem' on the experience of emptiness. *Being and Nothingness* has had, as the philosopher Mary Warnock shows, a unique status: becoming almost the definitive text book of Existentialism. As Warnock notes, the distinctiveness of *Being and Nothingness* lies in its methods of argument. Sartre turns every general question back towards the realm of particular experience. Thus the whole work has an existential texture. At this same time, Sartre joined the Resistance, belonging to a group called 'Socialism and Liberty'.

There is a unique urgency to Sartre's philosophical and literary voices of the late 1930s and 1940s. All meaning remains to be determined, at any given moment. We look out, as Sartre's hero Mathieu does in *The Reprieve*, and see 'a space of a hundred million dimensions'.

see also...

Appearances; Reality

Shame

There are several feelings which you can have when you aren't happy about how others see you. One is embarrassment, the feeling that you look out of place, that something you said or did belongs elsewhere. Embarrassment is about falling out of the cosy 'we' back into the chilly 'they'. Being embarrassed is a social event: you share enough of this group's tastes to understand why they recoil, yet you can't help seeming tasteless.

'Shame' also involves a sense of what others think, but it is far more internal, and goes far deeper. I wouldn't feel shame if I turned up at the formal meeting wearing the wrong kind of sweater, only embarrassment. But I would feel shame if the meeting judged me to have falsified the accounts, and I accepted the judgement. Embarrassment belongs to the world of surfaces: you suddenly see how you look to them, and how you should look. In shame, you take into yourself a hostile judgement on your own acts or character. Finally, I am ashamed in my own presence. As Sartre says, 'Shame ... realizes an intimate relation of myself to myself.' I stand accused before my own unrelenting judgement, which stands in for the condemnation of the world. Shame is intimate, the quiet and inescapable voice of your own values. In Sartre's existential shame, I suddenly see myself to the heart: so, that is how I am, whereas in embarrassment you suddenly realize that is how I seem.

One of the great images of shame occurs in the biblical Book of Job, a text which preoccupies many Existentialists, from Kierkegaard to Tillich, Buber and Derrida. Job has been cast down by God; he retained his sense of justification; but in the end another voice speaks:

'I have heard of thee by the hearing of the ear: but now mine eye seeth thee. ... Wherefore I abhor myself and repent in dust and ashes.'   42:6–7

In this image, the voice of his shame is called 'the Lord', but it speaks from close up, from inside.

see also...

Justification; Others

Sincerity

'I am really really glad to be here,' says the guest, with a smile. Imagine a world where everyone was sincere all the time. How different would it be from this real one? The question is interesting because of what the answers reveal about our view of one another. Do we experience each other as open books or as obscure fragments requiring specialist interpretation?

According to Existentialism, total sincerity would be almost unrecognizably strange. In de Beauvoir's fiction, one character sarcastically accuses another of a 'reckless taste for sincerity', as if it were a dangerous extravagance. In his strange collection of sayings and paradoxes, *Human, All Too Human*, Nietzsche maps the terrain of insincerity. He notes ironically the 'benevolent dissimulation' with which each person acts as if he does not 'see through' all the others. From observing ourselves inwardly, argues Nietzsche, we can tell, if we are honest, that the others must also be holding back. Normal communication is a tacit conspiracy. Then there is our 'feigned sympathy', which is often only too obviously phoney, as a result of which, according to Nietzsche, we become even less sympathetic than we were in the first place. There is our 'false praise', which annoys us even more than insincere blame, because it forces upon us compromised standards.

To the extent that these are recognizable tactics, are we all then morally insincere and corrupt? Nietzsche takes us beyond this ethic of transparency. He adds that we all know only too well that 'language is not given us for the communication of feeling'. In other words, however hard we try, our emotions will not simply slip into the words we choose. There is always a gap between our true feelings and our expression. This is not because we are weak or wicked, but because language is by nature indirect. Words take off sideways, they do not move in straight lines. We are pulled away from our true emotions every time we reach for a word. No wonder a taste for sincerity is dangerous: it challenges language itself.

> **see also...**
>
> *Honesty; Irony*

Sisyphus

Freud gave us a Greek mythical hero to embody human suffering: he chose Oedipus to represent the unbearable truth. For Existentialism, Albert Camus chose Sisyphus, condemned by the Greek gods to heave a huge rock uphill in the underworld, and then eternally watch it roll back down, only to start all over again at the bottom. After Freud, Oedipus is the luckless victim of the unconscious: condemned innocently to fulfil unspeakable desires. What makes Sisyphus the existential alternative to represent the dark side of human experience?

Camus declares that Sisyphus is a hero, as heroic as his fate is absurd. He has been condemned, apparently, for scorning the gods, for loving life too much and refusing to return to the underworld from which he had been granted a temporary reprieve. But what interests Camus is the particular torment, the pointless labour 'in which the whole being is exerted towards accomplishing nothing'. Sisyphus represents the torment of a life lived as if to the full but without any point: his days not so much a bad life, as a terrifying parody of a truly good life. He acts

with his whole being, he makes himself into a positive presence in the world, and at the same time all this is turned into nothing, snatched away endlessly. Sisyphus lives for and through his work, and he acts as if this work were full of purpose: yet it goes nowhere.

But Sisyphus is not merely a victim. Camus pauses to watch his hero at the top of the slope. The rock has rumbled downwards. He is about to follow. Just for an instant, Sisyphus has a 'breathing space'. Sometimes, he must be dispirited, lost. But at other moments, he summons all his powers and then 'that is the hour of consciousness'. Poised before his descent, the Greek hero surveys his whole situation, he takes it all in, and then he goes down. In that moment, he makes himself free and even happy. Over the twentieth century stand the two heroes: Freud's Oedipus symbolizes the unconscious, Camus' Sisyphus symbolizes full awareness.

see also...

Consciousness; Hero

Solipsism

'Solipsism' means means the attempt to conceive of your own life without making any reference to anyone else (beyond yourself). Existentialism did not invent the idea of solipsism, which has ancient roots; but Sartre in particular gave a new colouring to the idea. For some commentators, such as Iris Murdoch, Sartre himself ran the risk of 'solipsism', of isolating the individual from all external contexts or relationships, trying to understand the human world in terms of separate actors called individuals. Sartre himself talked of 'The Reef of Solipsism', as if this were a hidden danger beneath the surface of the seas over which he sailed his philosophy. In other words, he recognized a need to show that he was not guilty of the philosophical and perhaps even moral sin of solipsism – that his existential philosophy had not run aground on this most treacherous of concealed dangers. Solipsism becomes one name for what might happen to Existentialism if it goes wrong.

Try a thought experiment. Think of yourself and your own characteristics. Give your qualities their names and try to keep out all reference to anyone else. Let's say you think of yourself as kind – but how could you know that without making any reference to other people? Or let's say you are patient. But how can you know that except in terms of experiences of being with others? Then imagine trying to say someone is 'loving' with no regard to others. That is what the solipsistic sense of the self would be like. In fact, Sartre writes with near-admiration of the effort 'to get rid of the concept of the Other completely'. It sounds like a liberation, which is a sign of how deeply individualist Sartre's Existentialism can become. Solipsism is for him an understandable goal.

In fact, his argument against Solipsism is strange. He argues that you would have to see yourself as the only real person: all the others are mere appearances. But only a god could reassure you that you are real and they are not: so you have now submitted to the gaze of another after all.

see also...

I; Others

Suicide

In 1942, the philosopher Karl Jaspers was trapped in his native Germany, living in terror with his Jewish wife, Gertrud, dismissed from his job, chronically ill. He wrote about the idea of suicide. On the one hand, he rejected the Christian rule that suicide is always wrong: in some cases, staying alive might be mere cowardice. On the other hand, he argued (with himself perhaps) that suicide committed to escape execution or torture is not a free act, but a mere 'deed forced upon one'. Suicide is a question which he cannot avoid, and yet which he refuses to resolve.

Jaspers' dilemma about suicide arises because he refuses to follow absolute rules, and asks the question: is this an authentic, free act, or is it a mere submission either to circumstances or the will of others? For Camus, after the war, the dilemma remained: 'There is but one truly serious philosophical problem and that is suicide.' If life has no inherent meaning, if there are no fixed rules, then why not choose death, as a final and pure decision? Camus, however, turns aside from this argument: it is too easy an answer to the predicament of an absurd world. In fact, for Camus, suicide is merely a way of accepting one's fate, since we are all going to die anyway. Suicide is the most abject submission to necessity, not a moment of freedom. On the contrary, Camus argues that if there is no meaning, then what counts is 'the quantity and variety of experience': to cut short experience is to limit the value of your life, and of life itself. The Existentialist should be able to see, unclouded by abstract ideals, that '20 years of life' is always an offer worth taking, more is always better than less.

Existentialism gives no single way of answering the question of suicide. Jaspers and Camus share a refusal to argue from fixed rules or dogmas: the question must be faced. But, for all its gloomy tendencies, Existentialism tends to overleap the darkness of self-surrender.

see also...
Absurd; Freedom

Superman, The

Existentialism is not a moderate approach to life. In their different ways, the major Existentialists have tended towards different extremes. Probably the most notorious of all the extreme ideas developed within Existentialism is 'The Superman', a concept promoted by the philosophy of Nietzsche. We meet Nietzsche's 'superman' as part of the teaching of a character called Zarathustra, mouthpiece of many of Nietzsche's more provocative doctrines. Zarathustra has encountered a crowd waiting to see a famous tightrope walker. Instead they hear a sermon by Nietzsche's existential prophet. In this diatribe, Zarathustra declares that he has a message for them: 'I teach you the Superman.' It sounds sinister, and indeed the Superman became mixed in with the slogans of Nazism three decades later. Is the Superman an ideal of supreme force and absolute domination? In fact, Zarathustra defines the Superman as an open-ended ideal, which every person must create for themselves: 'Man is something that should be overcome. What have you done to overcome him?' The Superman is simply the goal of moving beyond current limits, exploring new possibilities of human experience.

Nietzsche himself did display a number of crude prejudices characteristic of his time and class, but there is nothing inherently fascist in the idea of the Superman. On the contrary, as Zarathustra argues, the Superman is a name for the refusal to accept conventional limitations and a demand for new experiments in living. The Superman is a name for whatever goes beyond complacent definitions: 'All creatures hitherto have created something beyond themselves: and do you want to be the ebb of this great tide, and return to the animals rather than overcome man?'

Nietzsche means the Superman to be a question not an answer. The question is asked of the present in the name of the future: do you really believe this situation is fixed by eternal laws?

see also...

Commitment; Value

94

Therapy

Therapy is one of the major ideas which the twenty-first century inherits from its predecessor. In existential terms, therapy expresses the ideal of the return to becoming, a defiance of pre-defined limits. Therapy suggests that we can re-make ourselves from within our deeply conditioned lives. Existentialists have contributed richly to the general idea of therapy, as well as offering particular therapeutic methods and ideas. Existentialism has also been deeply critical of certain common assumptions associated with therapy, particularly the idea of a passive patient being interpreted from outside or above. Therefore, Existentialists, from Sartre onwards, have been resistant to some of the more abstruse jargons by which therapies have put themselves above or beyond ordinary understanding.

Sartre developed an elaborate theory of 'existential psychoanalysis'. He started by rejecting the idea of fixed character types and even 'hereditary dispositions'. He also resisted the Freudian idea of the 'unconscious'. Instead he saw the role of the therapist as helping to discover an 'original choice', an orientation out of which a whole life has been determined or misshapen. No one can, however, define their own choice in isolation: it is only through the reflective power of another that our choice is made visible to us. We are the 'choice of being': we need another's presence to begin recognizing and changing this choice.

R D Laing evolved a practice of 'existential psychiatry', using Sartre's psychoanalytic insights. At the heart of Laing's therapy is 'relatedness', the power of entering into a relation which belongs, in a different way, to each individual. Laing seeks to recover and enrich this power of 'relatedness' in those whom it has become suppressed or damaged or shattered altogether. This means entering, as a therapist, into strange versions of the world, from the perspective of apparently lost individuals who inhabit destroyed landscapes. The concept of therapy is one positive possibility in the sometimes bleak worlds of Existentialism.

see also...

Existential Position; Relationship

Tillich, Paul

Paul Tillich (1886–1965) was one of the leading Protestant theologians of the twentieth century. By the advent of the Nazis in 1933, Tillich was an important figure in German intellectual and political life, a leader of a group of religious socialists. He held academic posts in Dresden and Frankfurt, but was banned from teaching early in the Nazi period and emigrated to America, where he worked at the New York Theological seminary, Harvard and Chicago. Tillich was an important figure in German anti-Nazism and gave radio broadcasts to Germany through the War. His thought was concerned with Christian faith in a modern situation, and he was deeply influenced by existential concepts, and by the work of his near-contemporary Martin Heidegger. Tillich's most influential writings were produced in English: *The Courage To Be* (1952), *The Dynamics of Faith* (1958) and *Systematic Theology* (1953–64). He gave many popular lectures, which form the basis of other publications, including *Love, Power and Justice* (1954).

The theologian John Macquarrie sees Tillich as a thinker who tried to extend the conception of God beyond traditional notions of religious systems or practices. Tillich was a major historian of Protestant theology in particular. In *Love, Power and Justice*, Tillich defines his central question as: 'What does it mean *to be?*' This exploration of being links Tillich most directly with other currents in Existentialism. For Tillich, the question always demands an affirmative response, yet he consistently confronts the darkest aspects of his century. In *The Courage To Be*, Tillich defined the central modern experience as that of 'meaninglessness', and he sought to renew our affirmation of ourselves 'in the face of' this crisis. Despite the unremitting bleakness of his diagnosis of the modern predicament, and his refusal of traditional consolations, many detected in Tillich's thought a source of cultural renewal. The theologian Richard Niebuhr found amidst the elements which Tillich himself called 'despair' a reaffirmation which he called the sense of God.

> ### see also...
> *Courage; Meaning*

Time

xistentialism has a way of dwelling on things which we usually ignore or take for granted. Attention stays with an experience which we are used to letting slip. It is this peculiar faculty of attending which makes Existentialism feel strange. One of the things which Existentialists have attended to most closely is time, and particularly our experience of time.

There are many Existentialist accounts of time. One of the most vivid is given in a recent work by the French writer and philosopher, Maurice Blanchot, in a work of poetic thought entitled *The Step Not Beyond*. Blanchot reminds us that communication itself presupposes that time can be trusted. I ask a question: 'Do you know how to drive this car?' You answer: 'I think so, but it isn't like mine.' As Blanchot sees: 'For there to be a play of questions and answers, time must keep its unitary structure with its three variables.' In other words, present, past and future must stay in their respective positions. My question comes before your answer, which in turn creates a space for a response up ahead. Blanchot, of course, has in mind more abstract dialogues: but the same logic applies: question and answer depend upon the stability of time itself.

But Existentialism sees time in terms of contrasting experiences. Blanchot also talks of 'the past being the infinitely empty and the future the infinitely empty'. In this eerie experience of time, there is no difference between what you said one minute past, and the remarks of legionaries in the Roman marketplace 2000 years earlier. Both are equally in the past, which is infinitely absent, out of reach, beyond. The same applies to the future: in a minute is as much not-here-yet as 2000 years ahead. But the present is consumed by these two infinities: one second ago vanishes as absolutely as 1000 years ago; one second ahead is as definitely not yet here as the next hundred years. Time may be the stable framework or the infinite void. Even where time is concerned, we are thrown back upon our own decisions.

see also...

Anguish; Heraclitus

Touch

When philosophy wants to describe how people discover their world, it usually talks in terms of sight. A person seeing an object: that is the typical way to represent human knowledge at its most basic. Existentialists also have lots to say about seeing and looking. But they do not pass over the other senses, and some of their most powerful discussions of knowledge and awareness concern touch, which others have viewed as more primitive than sight. Sartre's contemporary, the philosopher Maurice Merleau-Ponty, draws our attention to the strangeness of our two-handed touch. He starts with one hand, stretched out towards the outside world. I feel my hand from inside, he says, I am inside it as I hold out the fingers towards things. But now something weird happens. My other hand comes across and the two hands touch. Now I am inside both hands, but at the same time I feel each hand from the outside, as if it were just another object in the world. Merleau-Ponty calls this double touch a 'crisscrossing'. In his view, this twofold touch symbolizes our way of knowing ourselves and the world. At the heart of our experience is the recurrent moment when our awareness of the world doubles back on itself, in an 'intertwining'.

Why is this 'crisscrossing' so important? I pick up a cup with one hand. It is warm, say, and the night is cold, so I curl my other hand round too: the fingers meet on the far side of the cup. I am aware of myself from inside, of the cup as an object and of myself from outside. The moving hands 'incorporate themselves into the universe they interrogate': in other words, I discover myself in the act of discovering the world. Merleau-Ponty regards the two sensations as fitting together like the halves of a split orange. The comparison is neat, because the orange also suggests a globe or a world being put back together. In our hands, as they meet one another in the world, we understand how we belong to the world which we are exploring.

see also...

Ambiguity; Body

Tragedy

Existentialism has been consistently preoccupied with ideas of tragedy, and always uneasy in the face of them. In *Fear and Trembling*, Kierkegaard defines his knight of faith, the figure of existential commitment, by a subtle contrast with the tragic hero. In tragedy, the hero faces terrible ordeals and sometimes appalling dilemmas and sacrifices. But for Kierkegaard, the tragic hero remains ethically admirable. On the other hand, the knight of faith is called upon to act in contradiction to our understanding of good and evil, the key example being Abraham's willingness to sacrifice his son in the Old Testament. Tragedy is the 'Other' of Existentialism here, the rival approach to a shared vision of suffering. The same type of contrast with tragedy can be discerned in the dramas of Samuel Beckett. Here Hamlet is reduced to Hamm, and his parents are relegated to dustbins instead of providing the plot of a tragic drama.

A different approach to tragedy develops from the work of Nietzsche. In his first book *The Birth of Tragedy* (1872), Nietzsche analysed Greek tragedy in terms of an insuperable contradiction between two principles, the Dionysian and the Apollonian, one ecstatic and the other intellectual. This contradiction created tragic drama and ultimately destroyed it. Here again tragedy is seen as a philosophical vision, sharing many existential characteristics, and indeed this definition is part of Nietzsche's journey towards an existential approach. This approach to tragedy reappears in the thought of the Christian Existentialist Berdyaev. He sees a 'tragic conflict between Christianity and history'. This contradiction, like the Dionysian and Apollonian, cannot be resolved, at least not in this world. Through this conflict, 'each judges the other'. For History, Christianity is a failure, because it has not brought rebirth or prevented atrocity, over and over. But for Christianity, History is the force which has prevented the fulfilment of the truth on earth. Yet Berdyaev goes on to try to reach beyond, towards a future where Christianity becomes a new religion. For all these existential thinkers and writers, their personal vision is defined in the face of tragedy.

see also...

Hero; Sacrifice

Value

For some people values always seem to come from the past. The best you can hope for is to prevent the loss of these values, which everybody once shared. One could call this the 'already' view of values: they are already created, waiting to be either inherited or lost. The phrase 'family values' is an example of the 'already' school: they can be lost, or eroded, or forgotten, or, if we do well, they can be passed on to our children. Another example might be certain ideals of local community. There was a time when people around here shared an idea of community; but those values are under threat from new changes. There is no one political or religious viewpoint associated with this idea of value as an inheritance or a loss. Socialists and conservatives, fundamentalists and liberals can all use the 'already-there' idea of values.

Existentialism has an opposing idea of values. For Existentialists values are 'not yet': they are in the process of recreation, we are always reaching towards our values. The most polemical and influential account of the 'not-yetness' of values comes in Nietzsche's *Thus Spake Zarathustra*.

Nietzsche's existential prophet tells a parable in which there appears a dragon with shining scales: 'values, thousands of years old, shine on these scales ...' Each scale has another 'thou shalt' on it. According to this dragon, 'All value has long been created'. Change can only be the loss of values. In the parable, the lion stands against the dragon. But the lion is not simply the reverse of the dragon of created values. It would be a contradiction for the lion to embody new values, since they would then be as fixed as the old values. The lion represents the possibility of creating new values: 'To create new values – that even the lion cannot do.' But the lion encourages us to create 'freedom' within which we can begin to reach towards new values. Not-yet values do not belong to any one political party or theory; they seem to reach beyond conventional politics and morality.

see also...

Creativity; Freedom

World

'Why was the phenomenon of the world passed over?' With this strange-sounding question, Heidegger confronted the previous 2000 years of Western philosophy, from Plato to the nineteenth century. What did he mean? How could the world itself be overlooked by anyone, let alone by the most serious thinkers of a whole civilization?

Various concepts are built into Heidegger's question. First, he thinks of the world as being 'a phenomenon', in other words an entity with its own being, something which exists just as other things (and people) do. Therefore, the world is not merely the accumulation of everything else that we experience or encounter. Beyond all the objects and every person, including 'me', there is a world. Previous philosophy, claims Heidegger, has not noticed that the world is there, apart from all else. However thoroughly you took account of everything else, however impressive your logic, you would never arrive at this phenomenon called the world. It has to be recognized in its own terms. But how can philosophy have 'passed over' such a thing as the whole world? The answer is ironic. We never have any experience or thought without that world already being a part of it: so unless you pause and reflect, you will always have already taken it for granted. As our consciousness awakes into life, 'something like the world is already revealed to it', and so this world never seems to invite consideration in the first place. Once this world has been recognized, there are immediately new questions. Karl Jaspers explored the different ways we could know about this whole world. One could analyse it as an 'alien' entity – almost scientifically. Or one could explore the sense of the world as part of being 'at home' there. The difference is rather like that between a well-informed tourist and a true inhabitant of a city. The tourist may well have more information, from the up-to-date guide, and he may have been places the locals never visit. But he will lack a true feel for the place as a whole.

see also...

Earth; Knowledge

Further Reading

Arendt, H, *The Human Condition*, 2nd ed (University of Chicago Press, 1998)

Arendt, H, *Men in Dark Times* (Harcourt, Brace, Jovanovich, 1968)

Beauvoir, S De , *The Blood of Others*, trans by Yvonne Moyse and Roger Senhouse (Penguin, 1964)

Beauvoir, S De, *The Ethics of Ambiguity*, trans by Bernard Frechtman (Citadel Press, 1996)

Beauvoir, S De, *The Second Sex*, trans by H M Parshley (Vintage, 1997)

Beckett, S, *Collected Shorter Prose* (John Calder, 1986)

Beckett, S, *Endgame* (Faber & Faber, 1958)

Beckett, S, *Waiting For Godot* (Faber & Faber, 1965)

Berdyaev, N, *Christian Existentialism*, selected and trans by Donald Lowrie (George Allen & Unwin, 1965)

Blanchot, M, *The Step Not Beyond*, trans by Lycette Nelson (State University of New York Press, 1992)

Byatt, A, *Iris Murdoch* (Longman, 1976)

Buber, M, *I and Thou*, trans by R Gregor Smith (T&T Clark, 1958)

Buber, M, *On Judaism*, edited by Nahum Glatzer (Schoken Books, 1995)

Camus, A, *The Fall*, trans by Justin O'Brien (Penguin, 1963)

Camus, A, *The Myth of Sisyphus,* trans. by Justin O'Brien (Penguin, 1975)

Camus, A, *The Outsider*, trans by Joseph Laredo (Penguin, 1983)

Danto, A, *Sartre* (Fontana, 1991)

Derrida, J, *Cinders* (University of Nebraska Press, 1992)

Derrida, J, *The Gift of Death*, trans by David Wills (University of Chicago Press, 1995)

Dobson, A, *Jean-Paul Sartre and the Politics of Reason* (Cambridge University Press, 1993)

Dostoyevsky, F, *Notes From Underground*, trans by Jessie Coulson (Penguin, 1972)

Fallaize, E, (ed), *Simone De Beauvoir: A Critical Reader* (Routledge, 1998)

Fanon, F, *Black Skin, White Masks*, trans by Charles Markmann (Pluto, 1986)

Fanon, F, *The Wretched of the Earth*, trans by Constance Farrington (Penguin, 1967)

Gordon, L (ed), *Existence in Black: An Anthology of Black Existential Philosophy* (Routledge, 1997)

Hannay, A S and G Monro (eds), *The Cambridge Companion to Kierkegaard* (Cambridge University Press, 1998)

Heidegger, M, *Being and Time*, trans by J Macquarrie and E Robinson (Basil Blackwell, 1962)

Heidegger, M, *The Concept of Time*, trans by W McNeill (Basil Blackwell, 1992)

Heidegger, M, *Basic Writings*, edited by David Farrell Krell (Routledge, 1993)

Jaspers, K, *Basic Philosophical Writings*, trans by E Ehrlich, L Ehrlich and G Pepper (Humanities Press, 1994)

Kierkegaard, S, *Fear and Trembling*, trans by Alastair Hannay (Penguin, 1985)

Kierkegaard, S, *Fear and Trembling and the Book of Adler*, Introduction by George Steiner, trans by W Lowrie (Everyman, 1994)

Kierkegaard, S, 'The Seducer's Diary' in *Either-Or*, trans by A Hannay (Penguin, 1992)

Kahn, C (ed and trans), *The Art and Thought of Heraclitus* (Cambridge University Press, 1979)

Kaufmann, W (trans and ed), *The Portable Nietzsche* (Penguin, 1954)

Kundera, M, *The Unbearable Lightness of Being*, trans by Michael Heim (Faber & Faber, 1985)

Laing, R D, *The Divided Self* (Penguin, 1990)

Laing, R D, *The Politics of Experience* (Penguin, 1967)

Macquarrie, J, *Existentialism* (Penguin, 1973)

Magnus, B and K Higgins, *The Cambridge Companion to Nietzsche* (Cambridge University Press, 1996)

Marcel, G, *Man Against Mass Society*, trans by G S Fraser (University Press of America, 1985)

Marcel, G, *The Philosophy of Existence,* trans by Manya Harari (Harvill Press, 1948)

Maritain, J, *Existence and The Existent*, trans by Lewis Galantiere and Gerald Phelan (University Press of America, 1987)

Merleau-Ponty, M, *The Visible and The Invisible*, trans by A Lingis (Northwestern University Press, 1968)

Murdoch, I, *The Black Prince* (Penguin, 1973)

Murdoch, I, *Existentialists and Mystics,* edited by Peter Conradi (Penguin, 1999)

Murdoch, I, *Sartre: The Romantic Rationalist* (Penguin, 1989)

Nietzsche, F, *Human, All Too Human,* trans by R J Hollingdale (Cambridge University Press, 1986)

Nietzsche, F, *Thus Spoke Zarathustra,* trans by R J Hollingdale (Penguin, 1969)

Nussbaum, M, *Love's Knowledge: essays on Philosophy and Literature* (Oxford University Press, 1990)

Rorty, R, *Contingency, Irony and Solidarity* (Cambridge University Press, 1989)

Safranski, R, *Martin Heidegger: Between Good and Evil,* trans by Ewald Osers (Harvard University Press, 1998)

Sartre, J P, *Being and Nothingness,* trans by Hazel Barnes (Routledge, 1958)

Sartre, J P, *Essays in Existentialism,* edited by W Baskin (Citadel Press, 1993)

Sartre, J P, *Iron in the Soul,* trans by Gerard Hopklins (Penguin, 1963)

Sartre, J P, *Nausea,* trans. by Robert Baldick (Penguin, 1963)

Sartre, J P, *The Age of Reason* trans by Eric Sutton (Penguin, 1961)

Sartre, J P, *The Reprieve,* trans by Eric Sutton (Penguin, 1963)

Tillich, P, *Love, Power and Justice* (Oxford University Press, 1954)

Tillich, P, *The Courage To Be* (Nisbet & Co, 1952)